Android Studio Application Development

Create visually appealing applications using the new
IntelliJ IDE Android Studio

Belén Cruz Zapata

BIRMINGHAM - MUMBAI

Android Studio Application Development

First published: October 2013

Production Reference: 1081013

Published by Packt Publishing Ltd.

Livery Place
35 Livery Street
Birmingham B3 2PB, UK.

ISBN 978-1-78328-527-3

www.packtpub.com

Cover Image by Sheetal Aute (sheetala@packtpub.com)

Credits

Author
Belén Cruz Zapata

Reviewers
Karan Kedar Balkar

Angel Ivorra

Pablo Pera Mira

Antonio Hernández Niñirola

Acquisition Editor
Saleem Ahmed

Commissioning Editors
Shaon Basu

Meeta Rajani

Technical Editors
Tanvi Bhatt

Tarunveer Shetty

Project Coordinator
Amey Sawant

Proofreader
Jonathan Todd

Indexer
Priya Subramani

Production Coordinator
Adonia Jones

Cover Work
Adonia Jones

About the Author

Belén Cruz Zapata received her Engineer's degree in Computer Science from the University of Murcia in Spain, specializing in software technologies and intelligent and knowledge technologies. She earned an M.Sc in Computer Science and is now working in her Ph.D on the Software Engineering Research Group from the University of Murcia.

Belén is based in Spain, although in the field of her Ph.D she is now collaborating with the Université Mohammed V-Soussi, in Rabat, as beneficiary of an Erasmus Mundus program. Her research is focused on the mobile world and cloud computing.

She has a special interest in the development of mobile applications and new technologies. In the past few years, she has worked as a mobile developer for several platforms such as Android, iOS , and the Web.

She maintains a blog at `http://www.belencruz.com` and you can follow her on Twitter: `@belen_cz`.

I would like to thank Packt Publishing for offering me the opportunity to write this book. I would particularly like to thank Reshma Raman, Meeta Rajani, and Amey Sawant for their valuable help.

I would also like to thank my mentors during the last months, Miguel R. and P. Salinas; my friends, especially Ana, Nerea, and the *yupi* group, for cheering me up; my family, especially my parents and brother, for supporting me; and finally my significant other for everything and more.

About the Reviewers

Karan Kedar Balkar has been working as an independent Android application developer for the past four years. Born and brought up in Mumbai, he holds a Bachelor's degree in Computer Engineering. He has written more than 50 programming tutorials on his personal blog (`http://karanbalkar.com`) covering popular technologies and frameworks.

At present, he is working as a Software Engineer. He has been trained on various technologies including Java, Oracle, and .NET. Apart from being passionate about technology, he loves to write poems and travel to different places. He likes listening to music and enjoys playing the guitar.

Firstly, I would like to thank my parents for their constant support and encouragement. I would also like to thank my friends, Srivatsan Iyer, Ajit Pillai, and Prasaanth Neelakandan for always inspiring and motivating me.

I would like to express my deepest gratitude to Packt Publishing for giving me a chance to be a part of the reviewing process.

Angel Ivorra is an autodidact software developer with 20 years of experience in several languages and platforms. He lives and works in Spain, in his own company (`http://www.crestasoftware.es`).

I would like to thank my wife and daughter for all the patience during my long nights working.

Pablo Pera Mira is an Android developer and entrepreneur. As a co-founder of Androidsx, Pablo has been involved in the design, development, marketing, and launch of more than 10 applications in the Google Play Store, with a total reach of over 10 million users.

He currently works for Pixable, where he leads the development of the Android application Photofeed, a product from Pixable, based in New York. He previously worked as a backend Java engineer for the control platform of LHC, the particle accelerator in CERN, in Geneva. His first contact with real-world software was at Google, Zurich.

Antonio Hernández Niñirola is a Computer Science Engineer and mobile applications developer, born and raised in Murcia in the southeast of Spain and currently living in Rabat, Morocco. He has developed several websites and also mobile applications that have been published in both the Google Play Market and the Apple Store.

After his degree in Computer Science, he pursued a Master's degree in Teacher Training for Informatics and Technology. Antonio pushed his studies further and is now a doctorate student under the Software Engineering Group of the Faculty of Computer Science of the University of Murcia and is actually a researcher for the University Mohammed Soussi V in Rabat.

As soon as Antonio got his first smartphone, a second-hand first generation iPhone, he started programming small applications as a form of entertainment. What started as a hobby, became a passion and is now leading his career both professionally and academically.

www.PacktPub.com

Support files, eBooks, discount offers, and more

You might want to visit www.PacktPub.com for support files and downloads related to your book.

Did you know that Packt offers eBook versions of every book published, with PDF and ePub files available? You can upgrade to the eBook version at www.PacktPub.com and as a print book customer, you are entitled to a discount on the eBook copy. Get in touch with us at service@packtpub.com for more details.

At www.PacktPub.com, you can also read a collection of free technical articles, sign up for a range of free newsletters and receive exclusive discounts and offers on Packt books and eBooks.

http://PacktLib.PacktPub.com

Do you need instant solutions to your IT questions? PacktLib is Packt's online digital book library. Here, you can access, read and search across Packt's entire library of books.

Why Subscribe?

- Fully searchable across every book published by Packt
- Copy and paste, print and bookmark content
- On demand and accessible via web browser

Free Access for Packt account holders

If you have an account with Packt at www.PacktPub.com, you can use this to access PacktLib today and view nine entirely free books. Simply use your login credentials for immediate access.

Table of Contents

Preface

Mobile applications have had a huge increase in popularity in the last few years and this interest is still growing among users. Mobile operating systems are available not only for smartphones but tablets as well, therefore increasing the possible market quota for these applications.

Android has characteristics that make it pleasant to developers such as open source and a certain level of community-driven development. Android has always been contesting with iOS (the Apple mobile system) in everything and with XCode, iOS presented itself as a more centralized development environment. The new IDE Android Studio makes this centralization finally available for Android developers and makes this tool indispensable for a good Android developer.

This book about Android Studio shows users how to develop and build Android applications with this new IDE. It is not only a getting started book but also a guide to advanced developers to build their applications faster and more productively. This book will follow a tutorial approach from the basic features to the steps to build for release, including practical examples.

What this book covers

Chapter 1, *Installing and Configuring Android Studio*, describes the installation and basic configuration of Android Studio.

Chapter 2, *Starting a Project*, shows how to create a new project and the type of activities we can select.

Chapter 3, *Navigating a Project*, explores the basic structure of a project in Android Studio.

Chapter 4, *Using the Code Editor*, exposes the basic features of the code editor in order to get the best out of it.

Chapter 5, Creating User Interfaces, focuses on the creation of the user interfaces using both the graphical view and the text-based view.

Chapter 6, Google Play Services, introduces the current existing Google Play Services and how to integrate them into a project in Android Studio.

Chapter 7, Tools, exposes some additional tools such as the Android SDK tools, Javadoc, and the version control integration.

Chapter 8, Debugging, shows in detail how to debug an application in Android Studio and the provided information when debugging.

Chapter 9, Preparing for Release, describes how to prepare your application for release.

Chapter 10, Getting Help, introduces how to get help using Android Studio and provides a list of online sites to learn more about the topics seen in this book.

What you need for this book

For this book you need a computer with a Windows, Mac OS, or Linux system. You will also need to have Java installed in your system.

Who this book is for

This book is not only a getting started book but also a guide to advanced developers who have not used Android Studio to build their Android apps before. This book is great for developers who want to learn the key features of Android Studio and for developers who want to create their first app. It's assumed that you are familiar with the object-oriented programming paradigm and the Java programming language. It is also recommended you understand the main characteristics of the Android mobile system.

Conventions

In this book, you will find a number of styles of text that distinguish between different kinds of information. Here are some examples of these styles, and an explanation of their meaning.

Code words in text are shown as follows: "We will go through the most important folders in our project, `build`, `gen`, `libs`, and the folders under `src/main`. "

A block of code is set as follows:

```
protected void onCreate(Bundle savedInstanceState) {
    super.onCreate(savedInstanceState);
    setContentView(R.layout.activity_main);
```

When we wish to draw your attention to a particular part of a code block, the relevant lines or items are set in bold:

```
    setContentView(R.layout.activity_main);

    if (savedInstanceState != null) {
        System.out.println("savedInstanceState = [" +
savedInstanceState + "]");
    }
```

New terms and **important words** are shown in bold. Words that you see on the screen, in menus or dialog boxes for example, appear in the text like this: "In the Android Studio welcome screen, navigate to **Configure | Project Defaults | Project Structure**."

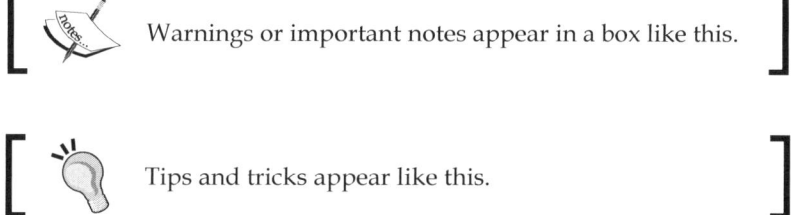

Warnings or important notes appear in a box like this.

Tips and tricks appear like this.

Reader feedback

Feedback from our readers is always welcome. Let us know what you think about this book—what you liked or may have disliked. Reader feedback is important for us to develop titles that you really get the most out of.

To send us general feedback, simply send an e-mail to feedback@packtpub.com, and mention the book title via the subject of your message.

If there is a topic that you have expertise in and you are interested in either writing or contributing to a book, see our author guide on www.packtpub.com/authors.

Customer support

Now that you are the proud owner of a Packt book, we have a number of things to help you to get the most from your purchase.

Downloading the example code

You can download the example code files for all Packt books you have purchased from your account at `http://www.packtpub.com`. If you purchased this book elsewhere, you can visit `http://www.packtpub.com/support` and register to have the files e-mailed directly to you.

Errata

Although we have taken every care to ensure the accuracy of our content, mistakes do happen. If you find a mistake in one of our books—maybe a mistake in the text or the code—we would be grateful if you would report this to us. By doing so, you can save other readers from frustration and help us improve subsequent versions of this book. If you find any errata, please report them by visiting `http://www.packtpub.com/submit-errata`, selecting your book, clicking on the **errata submission form** link, and entering the details of your errata. Once your errata are verified, your submission will be accepted and the errata will be uploaded on our website, or added to any list of existing errata, under the Errata section of that title. Any existing errata can be viewed by selecting your title from `http://www.packtpub.com/support`.

Piracy

Piracy of copyright material on the Internet is an ongoing problem across all media. At Packt, we take the protection of our copyright and licenses very seriously. If you come across any illegal copies of our works, in any form, on the Internet, please provide us with the location address or website name immediately so that we can pursue a remedy.

Please contact us at `copyright@packtpub.com` with a link to the suspected pirated material.

We appreciate your help in protecting our authors, and our ability to bring you valuable content.

Questions

You can contact us at `questions@packtpub.com` if you are having a problem with any aspect of the book, and we will do our best to address it.

1
Installing and Configuring Android Studio

You want to get familiar with the new and official Google IDE Android Studio. You want to know the features available in this environment. You would like to make your own Android applications, and you want these applications to be available to other users on Google Play Store. Can you do this easily? How can you achieve this?

This chapter will show you how to prepare your new Android Studio installation and how to take your first steps in the new environment. We'll begin by preparing the system for the installation and downloading the required files. We'll see the welcome screen that prompts when running Android Studio for the first time and we'll configure the Android **SDK (Software Development Kit)** properly so you have everything ready to create your first application.

These are the topics we'll be covering in this chapter:

- Installation of Android Studio
- Welcome screen when running Android Studio for the first time
- Configuration of the Android SDK

Preparing for installation

A prerequisite to start working with Android Studio is to have Java installed in your system. The system also must be able to find the Java installation. This can be achieved by setting an environment variable named JAVA_HOME, which must point to the **JDK (Java Development Kit)** folder in your system. Check this environment variable to avoid future issues during the installation of Android Studio.

Downloading Android Studio

The Android Studio package can be downloaded from the Android developer tools web page at: `http://developer.android.com/sdk/installing/studio.html`.

This package is an EXE file for Windows systems:

`http://dl.google.com/android/studio/android-studio-bundle-130.737825-windows.exe`.

A DMG file for Mac OS X systems:

`http://dl.google.com/android/studio/android-studio-bundle-130.737825-mac.dmg`.

Or a TGZ file for Linux systems:

`http://dl.google.com/android/studio/android-studio-bundle-130.737825-linux.tgz`.

Installing Android Studio

In Windows, launch the EXE file. The default installation directory is `\Users\<your_user_name>\Appdata\Local\Android\android-studio`. The `Appdata` directory is usually a hidden directory.

In Mac OS X, open the DMG file and drop Android Studio into your applications folder. The default installation directory is `/Applications/Android/ Studio.app`.

In Linux systems, unpack the TGZ file and execute the `studio.sh` script located at the `android-studio/bin/` directory.

If you have any problem in the installation process or in the following steps, you can get help about it and the known issues by checking *Chapter 10, Getting Help*.

Running Android Studio for the first time

Execute Android Studio and wait until it loads completely (it may take a few minutes). The first time executing Android Studio, a welcome screen will be prompted. As shown in the following screenshot, the welcome screen includes a section to open recent projects and a section of **Quick Start**. We can create a new project, import a project, open a project, or even perform more advanced actions such as checking out from a version control system or opening the configuration options.

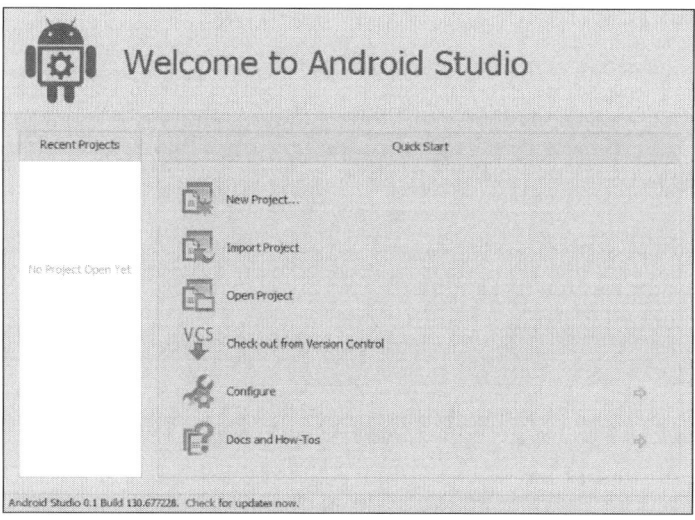

Let's have a look at the various options available in the **Quick Start** section:

- **New Project...**: Creates a new Android project
- **Import Project**: Creates a new project by importing existing sources from your system
- **Open Project**: Opens an existing project
- **Check out from Version Control**: Creates a new project by importing existing sources from a version control system
- **Configure**: Opens the configuration menu
    - **Settings**: Opens Android Studio settings
    - **Plugins**: Opens the plugins manager for Android Studio
    - **Import Settings**: Imports the settings from a file (.jar)
    - **Export Settings**: Exports the settings to a file (.jar)
    - **Project Defaults**: Opens the project defaults settings menu
    - **Settings**: Opens the template project settings. These settings are also reachable from the Android Studio settings (**Configure | Settings**)
    - **Project Structure**: Opens the project and platform settings
    - **Run Configurations**: Opens the run and debug settings

- **Docs and How-Tos**: Opens the help menu

  ° **Read Help**: Opens the Android Studio help, online version

  ° **Tips of the Day**: Opens a dialog with the tip of the day

  ° **Default Keymap Reference**: Opens an online PDF containing the default keymap

  ° **JetBrains TV**: Opens a JetBrains website containing video tutorials

  ° **Plugin Development**: Opens a JetBrains website containing information for plugin developers

Configuring the Android SDK

The essential feature that has to be correctly configured is the Android SDK. Although Android Studio automatically installs the last Android SDK available, so you should already have everything you need to create your first application, it is important to check it and to learn how we can change it.

In the Android Studio welcome screen, navigate to **Configure | Project Defaults | Project Structure**. In **Platform Settings**, click on **SDKs**. The list of the installed SDKs will be shown and you should have at least one Android SDK in the list. In **Project Settings**, click on **Project** to open the general settings for the project default template. You should have a selected **Project SDK** as shown in the next screenshot. This selected SDK is the default that will be used in our Android projects, but even so we can change it later for specific projects that require special settings.

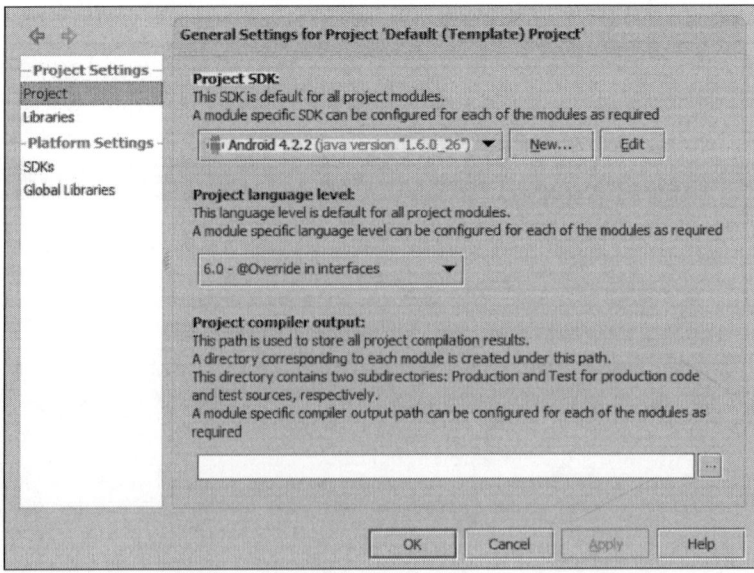

If you do not have any Android SDK configured in Android Studio, then we have to add it manually.

To accomplish this task, in **Platform Settings | SDKs** click on the green plus button to add an Android SDK to the list and then select the home directory for the SDK. Check if you have it in your system by navigating to your Android Studio installation directory. You should find a folder named `sdk` that contains the Android SDK and its tools. The Android Studio installation directory may be in a hidden folder, so click on the button highlighted in the following screenshot to **Show Hidden Files and Directories**:

If you want to use another Android SDK different from the one included in Android Studio, select it instead. For example, if you previously used the **ADT** (**Android Development Tools**) plugin for Eclipse, you already have an Android SDK installation in your system. You could also add both of them.

When you finish adding the SDK, it will appear in the list and you can select the default from the project settings.

>
> **Downloading the example code**
>
> You can download the example code files for all Packt books you have purchased from your account at `http://www.packtpub.com`. If you purchased this book elsewhere, you can visit `http://www.packtpub.com/support` and register to have the files e-mailed directly to you.

Summary

We have successfully prepared the system for Android Studio and installed our Android Studio instance. We ran the Studio for the first time and now we know the options available in the welcome screen. We have also learned how to configure our Android SDK and how to install it manually in case you want to use a different version. Fulfilling these tasks will leave your system with Android Studio running and configured to create your first project.

In the next chapter, we will learn about the concept of project and how it includes everything the application requires, from classes to libraries. We will create our first project and we will discuss the different kinds of activities available in the wizard.

2
Starting a Project

You just installed Android Studio and now you want to get familiar with its features. You want to understand the necessary fields when creating a project. You would like to know how to add an icon to your application and associate it on the project, and you are wondering how to create the main activity and which type of activity to choose. How can you achieve this using Android Studio?

The goal of this chapter is to create a new project with the basic content it should start out with. We will use the Android Studio wizard to create the project and we will go through the project configuration fields. We will choose a launch icon for our application and we will go through the different kinds of activities available in the wizard to pick as the main activity for our project.

These are the topics we'll be covering in this chapter:

- Creating a new project
- Creating your application icon
- Types of activities to choose as your main activity

Creating a new project

To create a new project, click on the **New Project** option from the welcome screen. If you are not in the welcome screen, then navigate to **File | New Project**. The new project wizard opens.

The first step of the wizard is enough to create a project, but if you check the **Create custom launcher icon** option, a second step is added to the wizard, and if you check the **Create activity** option, two additional steps are added. Check both of them.

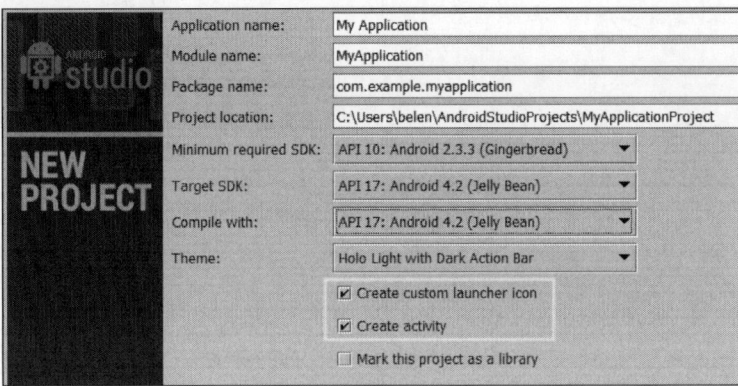

The fields that will be shown on the new project wizard are as follows:

- **Application name**: It is the name shown in Google Play and the one that users see.

- **Module name**: It is the name used only by Android Studio.

- **Package name**: Unique identifier of your application usually in the form `com.company_name.app_name` or `reverse_company_domain.app_name`. This form reduces the risk of name conflicts with other applications.

- **Project location**: It is the directory to save the project in your system.

- **Minimum required SDK**: It is the minimum SDK supported by your application. Devices with a previous SDK will not be able to install your application. Try to reach a balance between supported devices and available features. If your application does not require a specific feature published in the newest SDKs, then you can select an older **API (Application Programming Interface)**. The last dashboards published by Google about the platforms distribution show that 95.5 percent of the devices use Android 2.3 or superior. If you select Android 2.2, then the percentage rises to 98.5 percent. Official Android dashboards are available at `http://developer.android.com/about/dashboards/index.html`.

- **Target SDK**: It is the highest SDK that you have tested against your application. You should keep this value updated to the latest versions.

- **Compile with**: It is the SDK used to compile your application. This SDK is one of the SDKs you have installed and configured in Android Studio.

- **Theme**: Selects a default user interface theme for your application.

The option **Mark this project as a library** is used to create the project as a library module. A library can be referenced in other projects to share its functionality. Do not check this option.

Consider the fields shown in the previous screenshot. Select API 10 as the minimum SDK and API 17 as the target SDK. In the **Compile with** field, select the highest API version you have installed (API 17). Click **Next**.

Creating a custom launcher icon

This step allows you to create your application icon and will be shown if you checked the **Create custom launcher icon** option in the first step.

Android projects store several images resolutions to choose the most appropriate to the device screen resolution when the application is executing. To ensure that the icon will be displayed properly in every device, check if the XXHDPI image is not pixelated.

There are three options to create your application icon, an image, one of the provided cliparts, or a text. The most common is an image. You can select your own image file to create the icon and adjust some parameters such as its padding, its shape, or the background color. Choose the **Image** option and leave the default image and options as they are. Click on **Next**.

Choosing your type of activity

This step allows you to create the main activity of your application. This step will be shown if in the first one you checked the **Create activity** option.

Several types of activities can be selected:

- **Blank Activity**: This creates a blank activity with an action bar. The action bar includes a title and an options menu. The navigation type can be a tabbed user interface (tabs fixed or scrollable), horizontal swipe, or a drop-down menu. See more about action bars at `http://developer.android.com/guide/topics/ui/actionbar.html`.

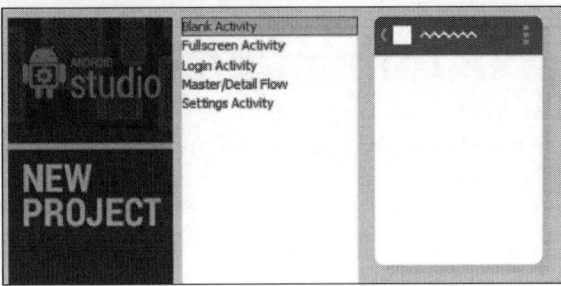

- **Fullscreen Activity**: This template hides the system user interface (such as the notification bar) in a full-screen view. The full-screen mode is alternated with an action bar that shows up when the user touches the device screen.

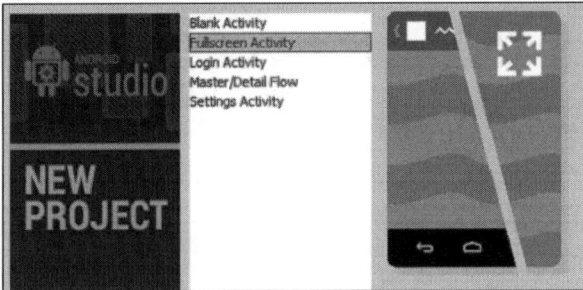

- **Login activity**: This template creates its view as a login screen allowing the users to log in or register with an e-mail and password.

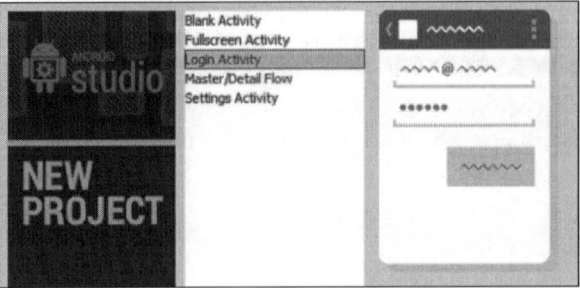

- **Master/Detail Flow**: This template splits the screen into two sections: a left menu and the detail of the selected item on the right. On a smaller screen, just one section is displayed, but on a bigger screen, both sections are displayed at the same time.

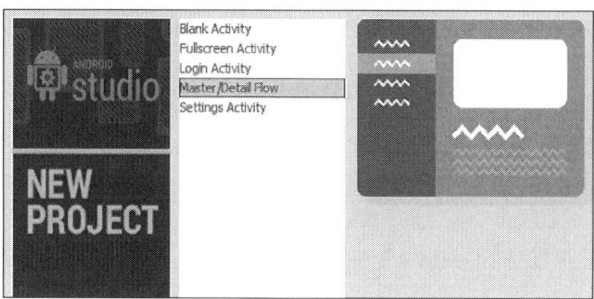

- **Settings Activity**: This creates a preference activity with a list of settings.

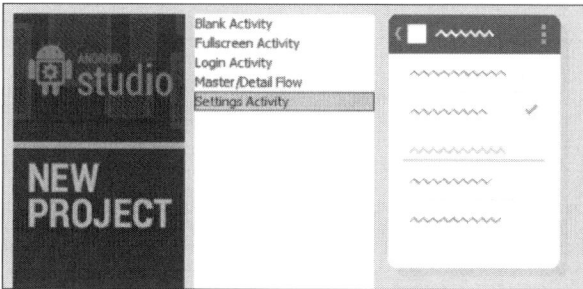

Select the **Blank Activity** and click on **Next**. In the last step, we can give a name to the activity and its associated layout. Leave the default values, select no navigation type, and click **Finish**.

Summary

We have used the Android Studio wizard to create our first project and we filled the configuration fields. We chose the launch icon for our application and made sure that it's going to display properly with any resolution. We went through the different kinds of activities.

In the next chapter, we will go through the different elements of the structure of Android Studio. We will find where we can create new classes, add and access libraries, and how to configure the project.

3
Navigating a Project

You just created your first Android Studio project and now you want to understand what is going on. You want to start programming, but before this you need to get familiar with the navigation of the project. How is everything structured? What settings can you change on the project? How can you change these settings and what do they mean?

This chapter is designed to introduce the structure of a project in Android Studio. We will start by understanding the project navigation panel. We will go through the most important folders in our project, `build`, `gen`, `libs`, and the folders under `src/main`, and we will learn how to change the project settings.

These are the topics we'll be covering in this chapter:

- Navigation panel
- Project structure
- Changing project properties

The project navigation panel

Initially in the main view of Android Studio, no project or file is displayed as you can see in the next screenshot. As Android Studio suggests, press *Alt + 1* to open the project view. You can also open it by clicking on the **Project** button from the left edge.

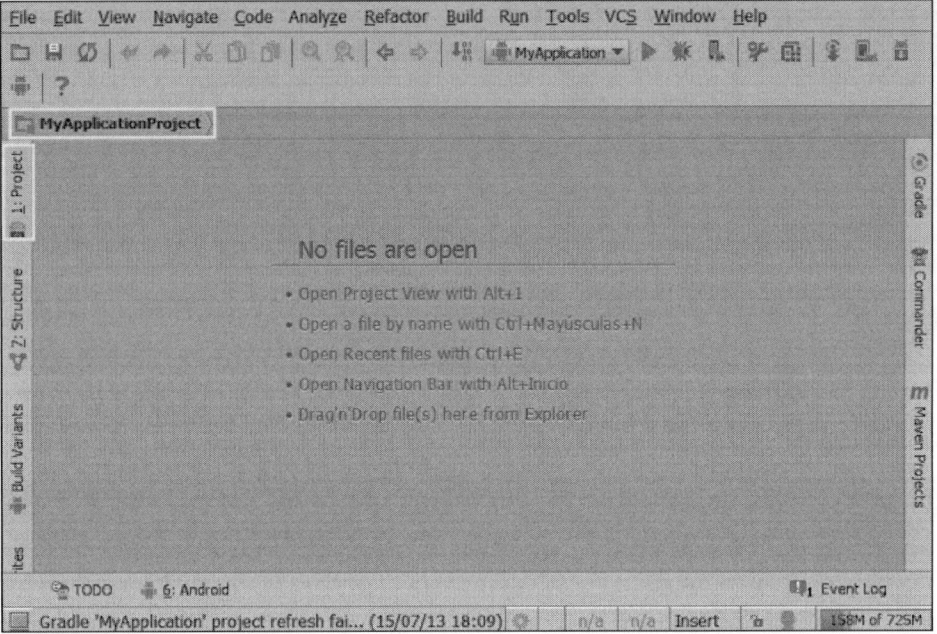

The project view shows the list of the open projects. The projects are displayed using a hierarchical view.

In the upper-left corner of the project explorer we can change the type of view: **Project** or **Packages**. The first one shows the directory structure of the project, while the second one shows only the package structure.

Chapter 3

In the upper-right corner there are some actions and a drop-down menu to configure the project view. These actions are highlighted in the following screenshot:

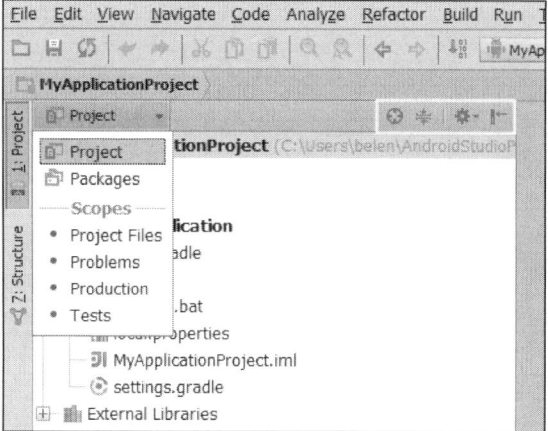

Click on the project name with the right mouse button to open the context menu, or click on any element of the project. From this menu we can:

- Create and add new elements to the project
- Cut, copy, paste, or rename files in the project
- Find elements in the project
- Analyze and reformat the code
- Build the project
- Compare files
- Open files in Explorer

Project structure

In the project navigation pane, we can examine the project structure. Inside the project structure is a folder with the name of our application. This folder contains the application structure and files. The most important elements of the application structure are:

- `build/`: A folder that contains the compiled resources after building the application and the classes generated by the Android tools such as the `R.java` file, which contains the references to the application resources.
- `libs/`: A folder that contains the libraries referenced from our code.

- `src/main/`: A folder that contains the sources of your application. All the files you will usually work with are in this folder. The main folder is subdivided as follows:

  ○ `java/`: A folder that contains the Java classes organized as packages. Every class we create will be in our project package namespace (`com.example.myapplication`). When we created our first project, we also created its main activity, so the activity class should be in this package. The next screenshot shows this main activity class inside the project structure:

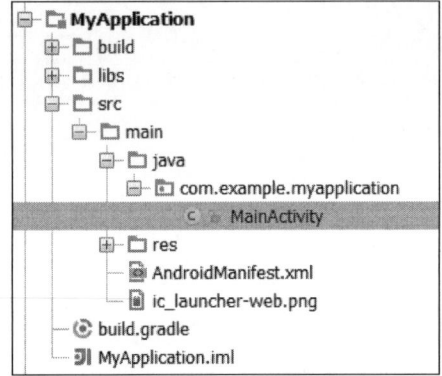

  ○ `res/`: A folder that contains project resources such as the XML files that specify layouts and menus or the images files.

  ○ `drawable/`: A folder that contains the images used in our application. There are different drawable folders categorized into the different screen densities. When we created our first project, we also created our application icon, so this icon is already in these folders named as `ic_launcher.png`.

  ○ `layout/`: A folder that contains the XML definitions of the views and their elements.

  ○ `menu/`: A folder that contains the XML definitions of the menus of the application.

  ○ `values/`: A folder that contains the XML files that define sets of name-value pairs. These values can be colors, strings, or styles. There are different values folders categorized into different screens options to adapt the interface to them. For example, to enlarge the components or the fonts when the application is running on a tablet.

- ° `AndroidManifest.xml`: This file is essential in an Android project and is generated automatically when we create the project. This file declares basic information needed by the Android system to run the application, package name, version, activities, permissions, intents, or required hardware.

- `build.gradle`: This file is the script used to build our application.

Project settings

There are two dialog boxes that contain project settings: **File | Settings** menu and **File | Project Structure**. Both are also available in the toolbar.

Select your project from the project view and navigate to **File | Settings** menu. In the left menu of the settings dialog, there is a section named **Project Settings [MyApplication]**. Some important options are:

- **Code Style**: Configures the default code style scheme.

- **Compiler**: Configures the Android DX compiler used when building our application.

- **File Encodings**: Changes the file's encoding. The default encoding is UTF-8.

- **Gradle**: It gives the Gradle's configuration. Gradle is a tool similar to Apache Ant and Apache Maven, based on Groovy to build and manage Java projects. Gradle is integrated in Android Studio.

- **Language Injections**: Adds or removes the available languages used in the editor.

- **Maven**: It gives the Maven configuration. Maven is a tool similar to Apache Ant and Gradle, based on XML to build and manage Java projects. Maven is integrated in Android Studio.

- **Version Control**: Configures the version control options. Version control will be explained in more detail in *Chapter 7, Tools*.

In addition to these settings, there are more of them in the project structure dialog. Navigate to **File | Project Structure** menu. The **Project Settings** are:

- **Project**: We can change the project name and the project SDK. Remember in *Chapter 1, Installing and Configuring Android Studio,* when we selected a SDK as the default one. In this screen we can change this SDK just for the current project.

- **Modules**: This screen shows a list of the existing modules with its facets. We can also remove them or create new ones. According to IntelliJ IDEA (`http://www.jetbrains.com/idea/webhelp/module.html`),

    A module is a discrete unit of functionality which you can compile, run, test and debug independently.

- **Libraries**: This screen shows a list of the libraries imported into the project. We can also remove them or add new ones. They will be added to the `libs/` folder.

- **Facets**: This screen shows a list of the existing facets. We can also remove them or create new ones. These facets were also displayed in the **Modules** view. According to IntelliJ IDEA (`http://www.jetbrains.com/idea/webhelp/facet.html`),

    Facets represent various frameworks, technologies and languages used in a module. They let IntelliJ IDEA know how to treat the module contents and thus ensure conformity with the corresponding frameworks and technologies.

Summary

We have learned how the projects are presented in Android Studio and what folders are in it by default once it is created. Now we understand the reasons for each folder and what `AndroidManifest.xml` is for. We went through the project settings both in the **File | Settings** and the **File | Project Structure** dialogs. By now, you should know how to manipulate and navigate a project in Android Studio.

In the next chapter we will learn how to use the text editor. A proper knowledge of the text editor is important in order to improve our programming efficiency. We will learn about the editor settings and how to auto-complete code, use pre-generated blocks of code, and navigating the code. We will also learn about some useful shortcuts.

4
Using the Code Editor

You have created your first project and you know how to navigate through the different folders, subfolders, and files. It's time to start programming! Have you ever wanted to be able to program more efficiently? How can you speed up your development process? Do you want to learn useful shortcuts to, for example, comment more than one line at once, find and replace strings, or move faster through different parameters in a method call?

In this chapter we will learn how to use the code editor and how to customize it in order to feel more comfortable when programming. It is worth knowing the basic features of the code editor in order to increase the developer productivity. We will learn about code completion and code generation. Finally, we will learn some useful shortcuts and hotkeys to speed up our development process.

These are the topics we'll be covering in this chapter:

- Customizing the code editor
- Code completion
- Code generation
- Find related content
- Useful shortcuts

Editor settings

To open the editor settings navigate to **File** | **Settings**, section **IDE Settings**, menu **Editor**. This screen displays the general settings of the editor. We recommend checking two options that are unchecked by default:

- **Change font size (Zoom) with Ctrl + Mouse Wheel**: This option allows us to change the font size of the editor using the mouse wheel, as we do in other programs such as web browsers.

- **Show quick doc on mouse move**: If we check this option, when we move the mouse over a piece of code and wait 500 ms, a quick doc about that code will be displayed in a small dialog. When we move the mouse again, the dialog automatically disappears, but if we move the mouse into the dialog, then we can examine the doc in detail. This is very useful, for example, to read what a method does and its parameters without navigating to it.

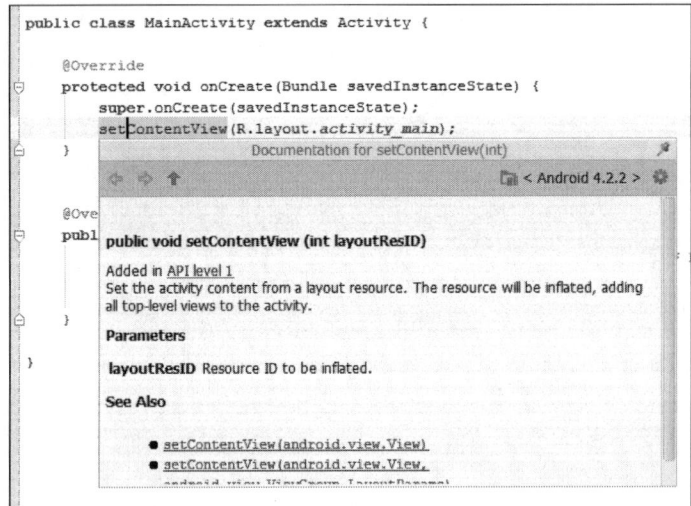

There are more settings distributed among seven categories:

- **Smart Keys**: Configures actions to be done automatically when typing, such as adding closing brackets, quotes or tags; or indenting the line when we press the *Enter* key.

- **Appearance**: Configures the appearance of the editor. We recommend checking the next two options that are unchecked by default:
    - **Show line numbers**: Shows the line numbers in the left edge of the editor. It can be very useful when we are debugging or examining the log.

- ○ **Show method separators**: Visually separates the methods of a class.

- **Colors & Fonts**: Changes the fonts and colors. There are a lot of options and elements to configure (keywords, numbers, warnings, errors, comments, strings, and so on). We can save the configurations as schemes.

- **Editor Tabs**: Configuration of the editor tabs. We suggest you select the **Mark modified tabs with asterisk** option to easily detect the modified and not-saved files.

- **Code Folding**: The **code folding** option allows us to collapse or expand code blocks. It is very useful to hide code blocks that we are not editing, simplifying the code view. We can collapse or expand the blocks using the icons from the editor or using the **Code | Folding** menu.

```
1    package com.example.myapplication;
2
3  ⊞ import ...
6
7    public class MainActivity extends Activity {
8
9        @Override
10 ⊕   protected void onCreate(Bundle savedInstanceState) {
11           super.onCreate(savedInstanceState);
12           setContentView(R.layout.activity_main);
13       }
14
```

- **Code completion**: Configures the code completion options. Code completion is examined in detail in the next section.

- **Auto Import**: Configures how the editor behaves when we paste code that uses classes that are not imported in the current class. By default when we do this, a pop up appears to add the import command. If we check the option **Add unambiguous imports on the fly**, the import command will be added automatically without our interaction.

```
1    package com.example.myapplication;
2
3  ⊟ import android.os.Bundle;
4    import android.app.Activity;
5  ⊟ import android.view.Menu;
6
7    public class MainActivity extends Activity {
8
9        @Override
10 ⊕   protected void onCreate(Bundle savedInstanceState) {
11   ? android.util.Log? Alt+Enter ete(savedInstanceState);
12           setContentView(R.layout.activity_main);
13           Log.i("MainActivity", "Test");
14       }
15
```

Code completion

Code completion helps us to write code quickly by suggestion lists and automatically completing the code.

The basic code completion is the list of suggestions that appears while we are typing. If the list is not displayed, press *Ctrl* + the Spacebar to open it.

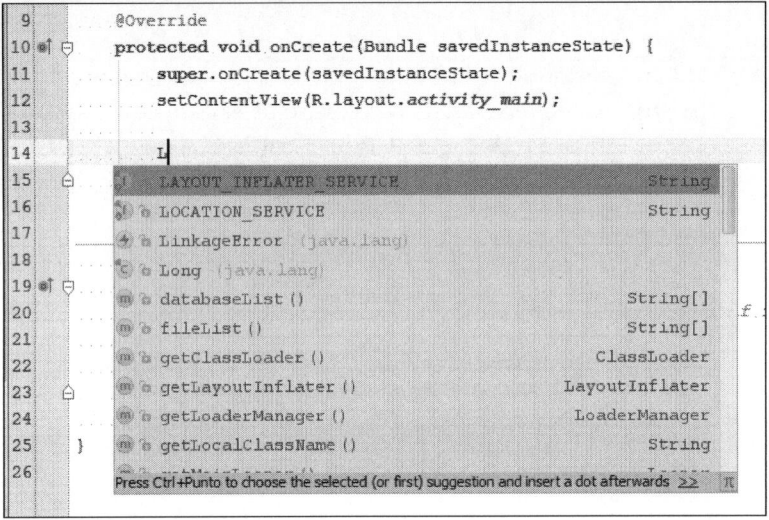

Keep typing, select a command from the list, and press *Enter* or double-click to add it in your code.

If the code we are writing is an expression, but we want to insert the expression in its negated form, when we select the expression from the suggestion list, instead of pressing *Enter* or double-clicking on it, press the exclamation mark key (*!*). The expression will be added with negation.

Another type of code completion is the **smart type code completion**. If we are typing a command to call a method with a String parameter, then just the String objects will be suggested. This smart completion occurs in the right part of an assignment statement, parameters of a method call, return statements or variable initializers. To open the smart suggestions list, press *Ctrl* + *Shift* + the Spacebar.

To show the difference between these two types of suggestion lists, create in your code two objects of different classes, String and int. Then call to a method with a String parameter, for example, the method i of the Log class. When typing the String parameter, note the difference between opening the basic suggestion list (*Ctrl* + the spacebar) as the next screenshot shows, and opening the smart type suggestion list (*Ctrl* + *Shift* + the Spacebar) as the screenshot on the next page shows.

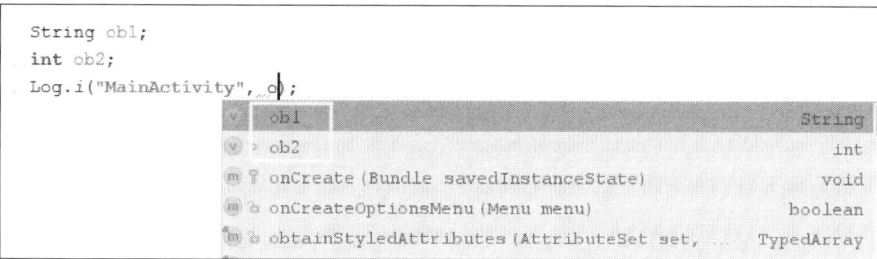

In the first list, which is shown in the previous screenshot, both objects are suggested although the int object does not match the parameter class. In the second one, which is shown in the following screenshot, just String objects are suggested.

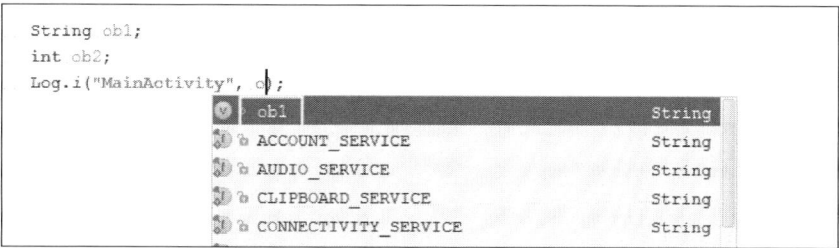

One last utility of code completion is the **completion of statements**. Type a statement, press *Ctrl + Shift + Enter,* and notice how the closing punctuation is automatically added. If you press those keys after typing the keyword if, the parenthesis and the brackets are added to complete the conditional statement. This shortcut can also be used to complete methods declarations. Start typing a method and after typing the opening parenthesis, or after typing the method parameters, press *Ctrl + Shift + Enter*. The closing parenthesis and the brackets are added to complete the method specification.

Code generation

To generate blocks of code in a class, navigate to **Code | Generate** or press the shortcut *Alt + Insert*. We can generate constructors, getters, and setters methods, equals and toString methods, override or delegate methods.

Another way to generate code is surrounding some of our code with some statements (if, if/else, while, for, try/catch, and so on). Select a code line and navigate to **Code | Surround With** or press *Ctrl + Alt + T*.

The third option is inserting code templates. Navigate to **Code | Insert Live Templates** to open a dialog box of the available templates. These templates can insert code to iterate collections, arrays, lists, and so on; code to print formatted strings, code to throw exceptions, or code to add static and final variables. In the left edge of the dialog, each template has a prefix, so if you type the prefix in the editor and press the *Tab* key, the code template is added automatically.

Try to type inn at the end of the onCreate method of our main activity and press *Tab*. A conditional block will appear. In this new block, type soutm and press *Tab* again. The result is shown next.

```java
protected void onCreate(Bundle savedInstanceState) {
    super.onCreate(savedInstanceState);
    setContentView(R.layout.activity_main);

    if (savedInstanceState != null) {
        System.out.println("savedInstanceState = [" +
savedInstanceState + "]");
    }
}
```

Navigating code

The most direct way to navigate to declarations or type declarations is to press *Ctrl* and click on the symbol when it is displayed as a link. This option is also accessible from **Navigate | Declaration**.

From the left edge of the editor we can navigate through the hierarchy of methods. Next to the method declarations that belong to a hierarchy of methods, there is an icon that indicates if a method is implementing an interface method, implementing an abstract class method, overriding a superclass method, or on the contrary, if a method is implemented or is overridden by other descendants.

Click on these icons to navigate to the methods in the hierarchy. This option is also available via **Navigate | Super Method** or **Navigate | Implementation(s)**. Test it by opening the main activity of our first project (MainActivity.java).

```
 6
 7      public class MainActivity extends Activity {
 8
 9          @Override
10  ⚡  Overrides method in 'android.app.Activity'  ndle savedInstanceState) {
11              super.onCreate(savedInstanceState);
12              setContentView(R.layout.activity_main);
13       }
14
```

Another useful utility related to code navigation is the use of custom regions. A **custom region** is just a piece of code that you want to group and give a name to. For example, if there is a class with a lot of methods, we can create some custom regions to distribute the methods among them. A region has a name or description and it can be collapsed or expanded using code folding.

To create a custom region we can use the code generation. Select the fragment of code, navigate to **Code | Surround With,** and select one of these two options:

- **<editor-fold…> Comments**
- **region…endregion Comments**

Both of them create a region but using a different style.

When we are using custom regions, we can navigate them using the **Navigate | Custom Region** menu.

The rest of the navigation options are accessible from the menu **Navigate**:

- **Class/File/Symbol**: Finds a class, a file, or a symbol by its name.
- **Line**: Goes to a line code by its number.
- **Last Edit Location**: Navigates to the most recent change point.
- **Test**: Navigates to the test of the current class.

- **File Structure**: Opens a dialog box that shows the file structure. Open the file structure of our main activity and observe how the structure is presented, displaying the list of methods, the icons that indicate the type of element, or the icons that indicate the visibility of the element.

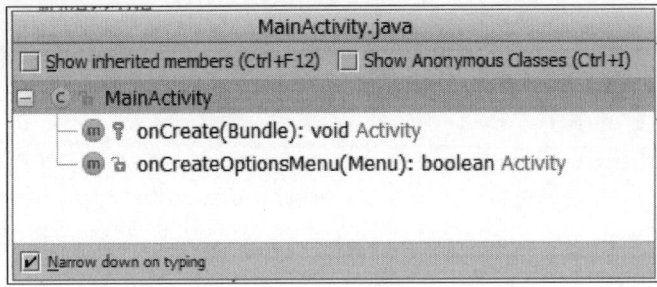

- **File Path**: Opens a dialog that shows the complete path to the file opened in the editor.

- **Type Hierarchy**: Opens a dialog that shows the type hierarchy of the selected object.

- **Method Hierarchy**: Opens a dialog that shows the method hierarchy of the selected method.

- **Call Hierarchy**: Opens a dialog that shows the call hierarchy of the selected method.

- **Next Highlighted Error**: Navigates to the next error.

- **Previous Highlighted Error**: Navigates to the previous error.

- **Next Method**: Navigates to the next method.

- **Previous Method**: Navigates to the previous method.

Useful actions

Some useful shortcuts are exposed in the following list:

- *Ctrl + W*: Selects the expressions based on grammar. Keep pressing these keys again and again to expand the selection. The opposite command is *Ctrl + Shift + W*.

- *Ctrl + /*: Comments each line of the selected code. To use block comments press *Ctrl + Shift + /*.

- *Ctrl + Alt + I*: Indents the selected code. Useful when you finish writing a block of code or method to clean it up.

- *Ctrl + Alt + O*: Optimizes the imports, removing the unused ones and reordering the rest of them.

- *Shift + Ctrl + Arrows*: Moves the selected code to another line.

- *Alt + Arrows*: Switches between the opened tabs of the editor.

- *Ctrl + F*: Finds a string in the active tab of the editor.

- *Ctrl + R*: Replaces a string in the active tab of the editor.

- *Ctrl + A*: Selects all the code of the opened file.

- *Ctrl + D*: Copies the selected code and pastes it at the end of it. If no code is selected, then the entire line is copied and pasted in a new line.

- *Ctrl + Y*: Removes the entire line without leaving any blank line.

- *Ctrl + Shift + U*: Toggles case.

- *Tab*: Moves to the next parameter.

Summary

By the end of this chapter, the user should learn some useful tricks and useful actions to make the most of the code editor. We know now how to use code completion, code generation, and some useful shortcuts for speeding up different actions. We have also customized our code editor and we are now ready to start programming.

In the next chapter, we will start creating our first user interface using layouts. We will learn how to create a layout using the graphical wizard and how to create it editing the XML layout file using the text-based view. We will create our first application, a classic *Hello World* example using the text view component. We will also learn about how to prepare our application for multiple screen sizes and adapt them for different device orientations. Finally, we will learn about UI themes and how to handle events.

5
Creating User Interfaces

Now that you have created your first project and have become familiar with the code editor and its functionalities, we will begin our application by creating our user interface. Is there more than one way to create a user interface using Android Studio? How can you add components to your user interface? Have you ever wondered how to make your applications support different screen sizes and resolutions?

This chapter focuses on the creation of the user interfaces using layouts. The layouts can be created using a graphical view or a text-based view. We will learn how to use both of them to create our layout. We will also code a *Hello World* application using simple components. We will learn about fragmentation on different Android-based devices and how to prepare our application for this issue. We will end this chapter with basic notions of handling events on our application.

These are the topics we'll be covering in this chapter:

- Existing layout editors
- Creating a new layout
- Adding components
- Supporting different screens
- Changing the UI theme
- Handling events

The graphical editor

Open the main layout located at `/src/main/res/layout/activity_main.xml` in our project. The graphical editor will be opened by default. Initially, this main layout contains just a text view with a **Hello world!** message. To switch between the graphical and the text editor, click on the bottom tabs, **Design** and **Text**.

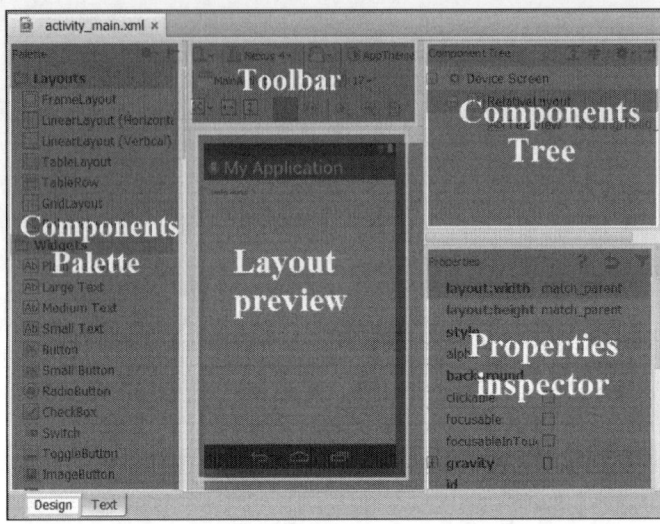

The toolbar contains some options to change the layout style and preview. The options of the toolbar are explained throughout the chapter.

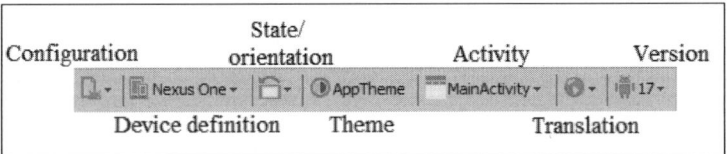

The components tree displays the components placed in the layout as a hierarchy. The properties inspector shows the properties of the selected component from the layout and it allows us to change them.

The palette lists the existing **UI** (**User Interface**) components to place in our layout. The palette organizes the components in different categories.

- **Layouts**: A layout is a container object to distribute the components on the screen. The root element of a user interface is a layout object, but layouts can also contain more layouts, creating a hierarchy of components structured in layouts. The recommendation is to keep this layout hierarchy as simple as possible. Our main layout has a relative layout as a root element.

- **Widgets**: Buttons, checkboxes, text views, switches, image views, progress bars, spinners, or web views are in this category. They are the most common components used in most layouts.

- **Text Fields**: These are inputs in which users can type text. The difference between them is the type of text users can type.

- **Containers**: These are containers group components that share a common behavior. Radio groups, list views, scroll views, or tab hosts are some of them.

- **Date & Time**: These are components related to date and time, as a calendar or clocks.

- **Expert**: These components are not as common as the ones in the widgets category, but it is worth taking a look at them.

- **Custom**: These are components that allow us to include our custom components, which are usually other layouts from our project.

The text-based editor

Change the graphical editor to the text editor by clicking on the **Text** tab.

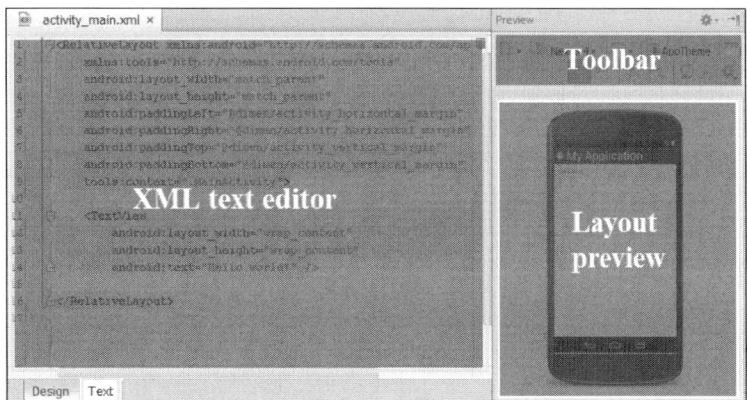

The toolbar is the same as the graphical editor. The preview displays the layout but it cannot be changed, you should use the design tab instead. The components are added to the layout using their XML declarations. The properties are also configured using the XML declarations. Like the graphical editor, the text editor shows just the text view element inside the root layout.

Creating a new layout

When we created our main activity, the associated layout was also created. This is a way to create a layout, while creating an activity.

If we want to add an independent layout without creating a new activity, then click with the right mouse button on the layouts folder (res/layout/) and navigate to **New | Layout resource file**. You can also navigate to the menu option **File | New | Layout resource file**. Type the filename and the root element.

Once the layout is created, the associated activity can be changed from the editor to another one. If the layout has no activity, any existing one can be linked to it from the editor. To accomplish this, in the toolbar of the layout editor, search for the activity option, click on it, and select the **Associate with other Activity** option. A dialog box that lists all the activities of your project will be opened so you can select one of them.

Adding components

Our main layout is a relative layout and contains a text view saying **Hello world!**, but let's add a new component. The easiest way to do this is using the graphical editor, so open the design tab. Select a component and drag it into the layout preview, for example, navigate to **Text Fields | Person Name** and place it below the text view.

In the component tree view, now there is a new `EditText` object. Keep the text field selected to examine its properties loaded in the properties inspector. Let's change some of them and observe the differences in the layout preview and in the component tree.

1. **layout:width**: Its current value is `wrap_content`. This option will adapt the width of the field to its content. Change it to `match_parent` to adapt it to the parent layout width (the root relative layout).

2. **hint**: Type `Enter your name` as the hint of the field. The hint is a text shown when the field is empty to indicate the information that should be typed. Due to the field having a default value, `Name`, the hint is not visible.

3. **id**: Its current ID is `@+id/editText`. This ID will be used from the code to get access to this object and is the one displayed in the component tree. Change it to `@+id/editText_name` to easily distinguish it from other text fields. Check that in the component tree the component ID has also changed.

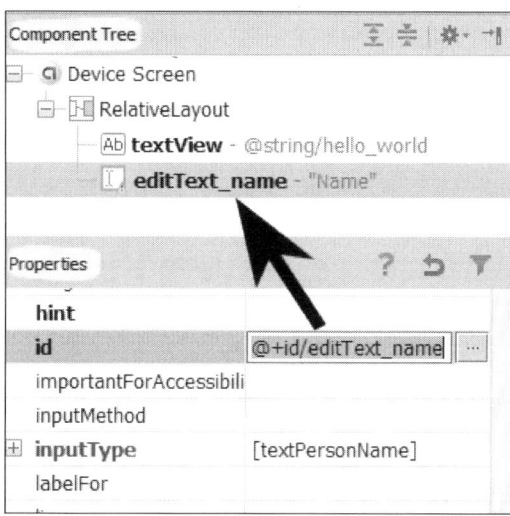

4. **text**: Delete the value of this field. The hint should now be visible.

If we switch to the text editor, we can see the XML definition of the text field with the properties we edited:

```
<EditText
android:layout_width="match_parent"
android:layout_height="wrap_content"
android:inputType="textPersonName"
android:ems="10"
android:id="@+id/editText_name"
android:layout_below="@+id/textView_greeting"
android:layout_alignLeft="@+id/textView_greeting"
android:layout_marginTop="15dp"
android:hint="Enter your name"
/>
```

From the text editor, the existing components and their properties can also be changed. Modify the text view ID (`android:id` property) from `@+id/textView` to `@+id/textView_greeting`. Having a descriptive ID is important since it will be used from our code. Descriptive variable names allow the code to be self-documenting.

Let's add another component using the text editor this time. Press the open tag key and start typing Button. Let the suggestion list appear and select a Button object. Inside the Button tag, add the next properties:

```
<Button
android:id="@+id/button_accept"
android:layout_width="wrap_content"
android:layout_height="wrap_content"
android:layout_below="@+id/editText_name"
android:layout_centerHorizontal="true"
android:text="Accept"
/>
```

Create the ID property with the value @+id/button_accept. Let the width and height adapt to the button content (wrap_content value). Place the button below the name text field using the android:layout_below property. We reference the name text field by its ID (@+id/editText_name). Center horizontally the button in the parent layout using the layout_centerHorizontal property. Set the text of the button (Accept).

The button is displayed in the layout preview. The next screenshot shows that if we switch to the graphical editor, the button is also displayed in it and in the component tree:

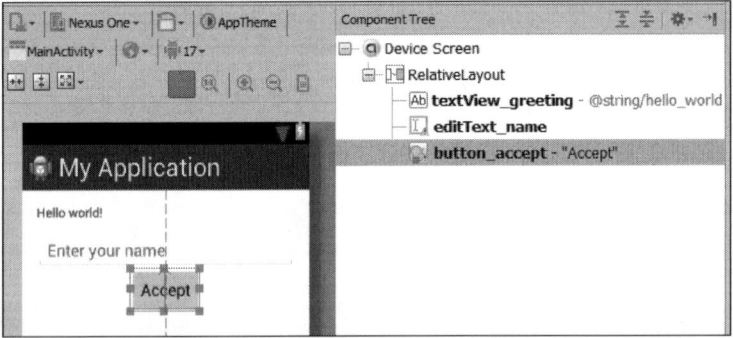

Supporting multiple screens

When creating an Android application, we have to be aware of the existence of multiple screen sizes and screen resolutions. It is important to check how our layouts are displayed in different screen configurations. To accomplish this, Android Studio provides a functionality to change the layout preview when we are in the design mode.

We can find this functionality in the toolbar, the **device definition** option used in the preview is by default **Nexus 4**. Click on it to open the list of available device definitions.

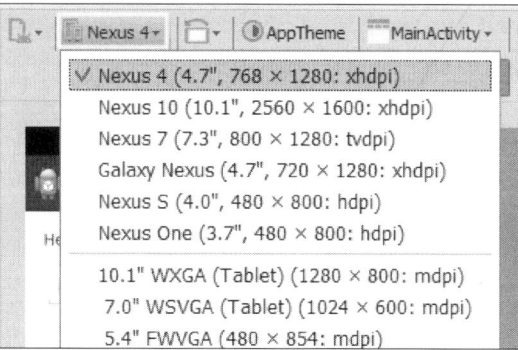

Try some of them. The difference between a tablet device and a device like the Nexus one are very notable. We should adapt the views to all the screen configurations our application supports to ensure they are displayed optimally.

The device definitions indicate the screen inches, the resolution, and the screen density. Android divides into ldpi, mdpi, hdpi, xhdpi, and even xxhdpi the screen densities.

- **ldpi (low-density dots per inch)**: About 120 dpi
- **mdpi (medium-density dots per inch)**: About 160 dpi
- **hdpi (high-density dots per inch)**: About 240 dpi
- **xhdpi (extra-high-density dots per inch)**: About 320 dpi
- **xxhdpi (extra-extra-high-density dots per inch)**: About 480 dpi

The last dashboards published by Google show that most devices have high-density screens (34.3 percent), followed by xhdpi (23.7 percent) and mdpi (23.5 percent). Therefore, we can cover 81.5 percent of the devices by testing our application using these three screen densities. Official Android dashboards are available at `http://developer.android.com/about/dashboards`.

Another issue to keep in mind is the **device orientation**. Do we want to support the landscape mode in our application? If the answer is yes, we have to test our layouts in the landscape orientation. On the toolbar, click on the layout state option to change the mode from portrait to landscape or from landscape to portrait.

In the case that our application supports the landscape mode and the layout does not display as expected in this orientation, we may want to create a variation of the layout. Click on the first icon of the toolbar, that is, the configuration option, and select the option **Create Landscape Variation**. A new layout will be opened in the editor. This layout has been created in the resources folder, under the directory `layout-land` and using the same name as the portrait layout: `/src/main/res/layout-land/activity_main.xml`. Now we can edit the new layout variation perfectly conformed to the landscape mode.

Similarly, we can create a variation of the layout for *xlarge* screens. Select the option **Create layout-xlarge Variation**. The new layout will be created in the `layout-xlarge` folder: `/src/main/res/layout-xlarge/activity_main.xml`. Android divides into *small*, *normal*, *large*, and *xlarge* the actual screen sizes:

- **small**: Screens classified in this category are at least 426 dp x 320 dp
- **normal**: Screens classified in this category are at least 470 dp x 320 dp
- **large**: Screens classified in this category are at least 640 dp x 480 dp
- **xlarge**: Screens classified in this category are at least 960 dp x 720 dp

A **dp** is a density independent pixel, equivalent to one physical pixel on a 160 dpi screen.

The last dashboards published by Google show that most devices have a normal screen size (79.6 percent). If you want to cover a bigger percentage of devices, test your application by also using a small screen (9.5 percent), so the coverage will be 89.1 percent of devices.

To display multiple device configurations at the same time, in the toolbar click on the configuration option and select the option **Preview All Screen Sizes**, or click on the **Preview Representative Sample** to open just the most important screen sizes. We can also delete any of the samples by clicking on it using the right mouse button and selecting the **Delete** option of the menu. Another useful action of this menu is the **Save screenshot** option, which allows us to take a screenshot of the layout preview.

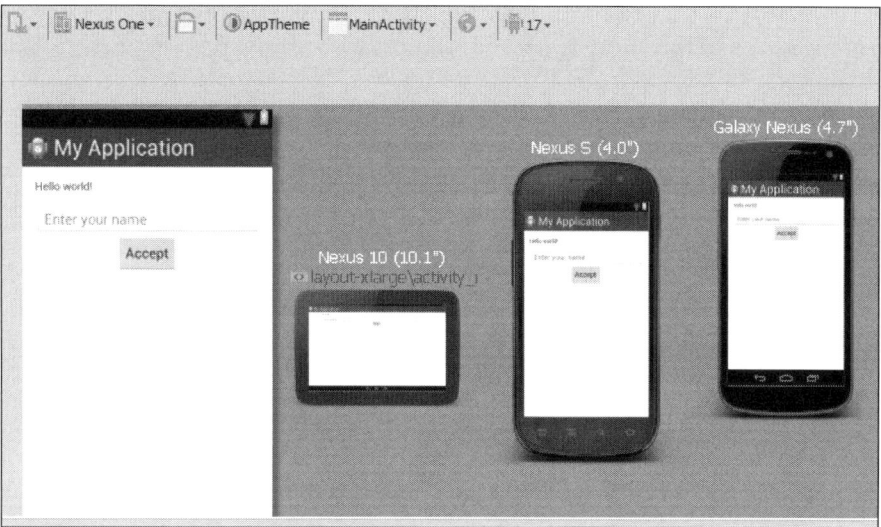

If we create some layout variations, we can preview all of them selecting the option **Preview Layout Versions**.

Changing the UI theme

Layouts and widgets are created using the default UI theme of our project. We can change the appearance of the elements of the UI by creating styles. Styles can be grouped to create a theme and a theme can be applied to a whole activity or application. Some themes are provided by default, such as the Holo style. Styles and themes are created as resources under the `/src/res/values` folder.

Open the main layout using the graphical editor. The selected theme for our layout is indicated in the toolbar: `AppTheme`. This theme was created for our project and can be found in the styles file (`/src/res/values/styles.xml`). Open the styles file and notice that this theme is an extension of another theme (`Theme.Light`).

To custom our theme, edit the styles file. For example, add the next line in the `AppTheme` definition to change the window background color:

```
<style name="AppTheme" parent="AppBaseTheme">
<item name="android:windowBackground">#dddddd</item>
</style>
```

Save the file and switch to the layout tab. The background is now light gray. This background color will be applied to all our layouts due to the fact that we configured it in the theme and not just in the layout.

To completely change the layout theme, click on the theme option from the toolbar in the graphical editor. The theme selector dialog is now opened, displaying a list of the available themes.

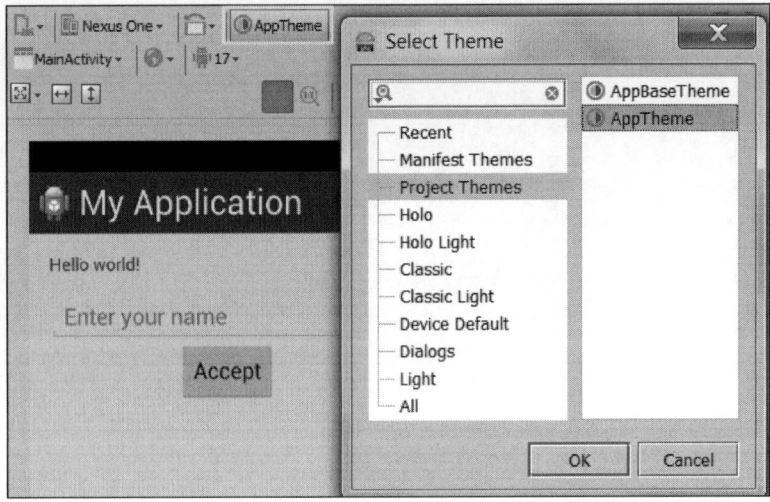

The themes created in our own project are listed in the **Project Themes** section. The section **Manifest Themes** shows the theme configured in the application manifest file (`/src/main/AndroidManifest.xml`). The **All** section lists all the available themes.

Handling events

The user interface would be useless if the rest of the application could not interact with it. Events in Android are generated when the user interacts with our application. All the UI widgets are children of the `View` class and they share some events handled by the next listeners:

- `OnClickListener`: Captures the event when the user clicks the view element
- `OnCreateContextMenu`: Captures the event when the user performs a long click on the view element and we want to open a context menu
- `OnDragListener`: Captures the event when the user drags and drops the event element
- `OnFocusChange`: Captures the event when the user navigates from an element to another in the same view
- `OnKeyListener`: Captures the event when the user presses any key while the view element has the focus

- OnLongClickListener: Captures the event when the user touches the view element and holds it

- OnTouchListener: Captures the event when the user touches the view element

In addition to these events and listeners, some UI widgets have some more specific ones. Checkboxes can register a listener to capture when its state changes (OnCheckedChangeListener), or spinners can register a listener to capture when an item is clicked (OnItemClickListener).

The most common event to capture is when the user clicks on the view elements. For this event, there is an easy way to handle it, using the view properties. Select the accept button in our layout and look for the onClick property. This property indicates the name of the method that will be executed when the user clicks on the button. This method has to be created in the activity associated with the current layout, in this case, in our main activity, MainActivity.java. Type onAcceptClick as the value of this property.

Open the main activity to create the method definition. An event callback method when a view is clicked has to be public, with a void return type, and it receives the view that has been clicked as a parameter. This method will be executed every time the user clicks on the button.

```
public void onAcceptClick(View v) {
  // Action when the button is pressed
}
```

From the main activity we can interact with all the components of the interface, so when the user clicks on the accept button, our code can read the text from the name field and change the greeting to include the name in it.

To get the reference to a view object, use the findViewById method inherited from the Activity class. This method receives the ID of the component and returns the View object corresponding to that ID. The returned view object has to be casted to its specific class in order to use its methods, such as the getText method of the EditText class to get the name typed by the user.

```
public void onAcceptClick(View v) {
  TextView tv_greeting =
    (TextView) findViewById(R.id.textView_greeting);
  EditText et_name = (EditText) findViewById(R.id.editText_name);

  if(et_name.getText().length() > 0) {
    tv_greeting.setText("Hello " + et_name.getText());
  }
}
```

In the first two lines of the method, the references to the elements of the layout are retrieved: the text view that contains the greeting and the text field where the user can type a name. The components are found by its ID, the same ID we indicated in the properties of the element in the layout file. All the IDs of resources are included in the R class. The R class is autogenerated in the build phase and we must not edit it. If this class is not autogenerated, then probably some file of our resources contains an error.

The next line is a conditional statement to check that the user typed a name, a case in which the text will be replaced by a new greeting that contains that name. In the next chapters we will learn how to execute our application in an emulator and we will be able to test this code.

In case the event we want to handle is not the user click, then we have to create and add the listener by code in the onCreate method of the activity. There are two options:

- Implement the listener interface in the activity and then add the unimplemented methods. The methods required by the interface are the methods to receive the events.

- Create a private anonymous implementation of the listener in the activity file. The methods that receive the events are implemented in this object.

Finally, the listener implementation has to be assigned to the view element using the setter methods, setOnClickListener, setOnCreateContextMenu, setOnDragListener, setOnFocusChange, setOnKeyListener, and so on. The listener assignment is usually included in the onCreate method of the activity. If the listener was implemented directly by the activity, then the parameter indicated to the setter method is its own activity using the keyword this as the following code shows:

```
Button b_accept = (Button) findViewById(R.id.button_accept);
b_accept.setOnClickListener(this);
```

The activity should then implement the listener and the onClick method required by the listener interface.

```
public class MainActivity extends Activity
implements View.OnClickListener {
  @Override
  public void onClick(View view) {
    // Action when the button is pressed
  }
```

Summary

By the end of this chapter, we have learned how to create and edit the user interface layouts by using both the graphical and the text-based editors. We finished our first small application and we have upgraded it with some basic components. The user should now be able to create a simple layout and to test it with different styles, screens sizes and screen resolutions. We have also learned about the different available UI themes and finally, we have learned about events and how to handle them using listeners.

In the next chapter we will learn about Google Play available services and how to integrate them into our project using Android Studio. We will learn how to install and integrate different libraries available with Google technology such as Google Maps, Google Plus, and more.

6
Google Play Services

Now that you have become familiar with the use of components on layouts, you should start thinking about extra functionality. Google Play Services give you features to attract users using Google features such as Google Maps, Google+, and more. How can you easily add these features to your application? What features are available? What are the Android version requirements to use Google Play Services?

This chapter focuses on the creation, integration, and use of Google Play Services using Android Studio. We will learn about which Google services are available. We will also learn about the standard authorization API in order to have a safe way to grant and receive access tokens to Google Play Services. We will also learn about the limitations of these services and the benefits of using them.

These are the topics we'll be covering in this chapter:

- Existing Google Services
- Adding Google Play Services from the IDE
- Integrating Google Play Services in your app
- Understanding automatic updates
- Using Google Services in your app

How Google Play Services work

When Google previewed Google Play Services at Google I/O 2012, it said that the platform (`https://developers.google.com/events/io/2012/`)...

> *...consists of a services component that runs on the device and a thin client library that you package with your app.*

This means that Google Play Services work thanks to two main components: the Google Play Services client library and the Google Play Services APK.

- **Client library**: The Google Play Services client library includes the interfaces to each Google Service that is used by your app. The library is included when you pack your app and it allows your users to authorize the app with access to these services using their credentials. The client library is upgraded from time to time by Google, adding new features and services. You may upgrade the library in your app through an update to your app, although it is not necessary if you are not including any of the new features.

- **Google Play Services APK**: The Google Play Services **Android Package (APK)** runs as a background service in the Android operating system. Using the client library, your app accesses this service, which is the one that carries out the actions during runtime. The APK is not guaranteed to be installed on all devices. In case the device does not come with it installed, the APK is available in the Google Play Store.

This way, Google manages to separate the runtime of its services from the implementation you do as a developer, so you do not need to upgrade your application every time Google Play Services are upgraded.

Although Google Play Services are not included in the Android platform itself, they are supported by most Android-based devices. Any Android device running Android 2.2 or newer is ready to install any application that uses Google Play Services.

Services available

Google Play Services are thought to easily add more features to attract users on a wide range of devices while using well-known features powered by Google. Using these services, you can add new revenue sources, manage the distribution of the app, access statistics and learn about your application's users customs, and improve your application with easy to implement Google features such as maps or Google's social network, Google+. The services are explained as follows:

- **Games**: Using this Google Play Game Service, you can improve your game with a more social experience.

- **Location**: Integrating the location APIs, you can make your application location-aware.

- **Google Maps**: Google Maps API allows you to use the maps provided by Google in your application and to customize them.

- **Google+**: Using Google+ Platform for Android, you can authenticate the user of your app. Once authenticated, you can also access their public profile and social graph.

- **In-app Billing**: Selling digital content from your apps is possible using Google Play In-app Billing. You can use this service to sell one-time billing or temporal subscriptions to premium services and features.

- **Cloud Messaging**: **Google Cloud Messaging (GCM)** for Android allows you to exchange data between the app running in an Android-based device and your server.

- **Panorama**: It enables the user to see a 360-degree panorama picture.

Adding Google Play Services to Android Studio

The first thing we need to know is what we need to add to our Android Studio. We have just learned that the APK is available in Google Play Store and it is the actual runtime of the services. We, as developers, only need this package to be available in our testing device while debugging our application. What we need to add to Android Studio is the Google Play Services client library.

This library is distributed through the Android SDK Manager (Software Development Kit Manager), which will be explained in detail in *Chapter 7, Tools*. To open it, navigate to **Tools** | **Android** | **SDK Manager**. We can find Google Play Services in the packages list under the folder **Extras**. Select the **Google Play Services** checkbox and click on the **Install 1 package...** button.

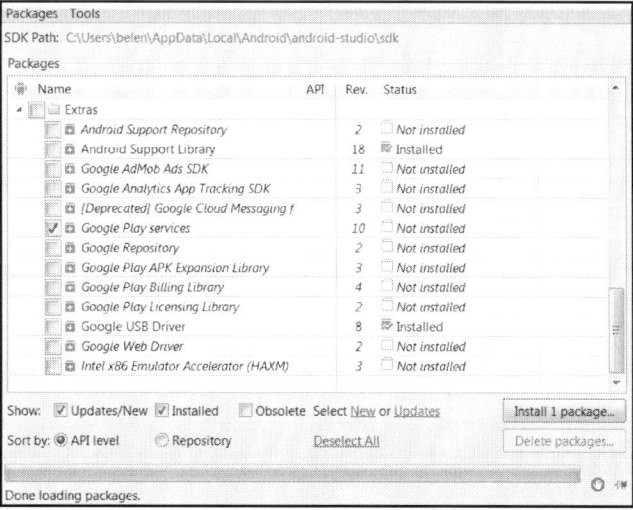

Performing these actions will add the library project into the location of our SDK installation folder, `/sdk/extras/google/google_play_services/`. You can check the exact path by hovering the mouse over the Google Play Services row in the SDK manager and looking at the tool tip.

Packages				
🤖 Name	API	Rev.	Status	
☐ 🗂 Google Analytics App Tracking SDK		3	☐ Not installed	
☐ 🗂 [Deprecated] Google Cloud Messaging f		3	☐ Not installed	
☐ 🗂 Google Play services		10	☑ Installed	

Google Play services, revision 10
By Google Inc.
Google Play Services client library and sample code
Location: C:\Users\belen\AppData\Local\Android\android-studio\sdk\extras\google\google_play_services
Installed from dl-ssl.google.com

Show: ☑ U

Sort by: ⦿ API level   ⦾ Repository   Deselect All   Delete package

Navigate to the library folder to examine its content. The `samples` folder contains sample projects of the authentication service (`auth/`), the Google Maps v2 service (`maps/`), the Google+ service (`plus/`), and the Panorama service (`panorama/`). The folder that contains the Google Play Services library project is `libproject/`. In this project folder is where the `google-play-services.jar` file is placed, `libproject/ google-play-services_lib/libs/ google-play-services.jar`.

Add this JAR file to your project by just dragging it into the `libs/` folder. Once this is done, select the JAR file and press the right mouse button on it. Select the **Add as Library** option. In the **create library** dialog, select the project library level, select your application module, and click on **OK**.

You now have the `google-play-services.jar` file available in your project libraries, under the `libs/` folder, and you will now be able to reference Google Play Services from your code.

Finally, you will need to add the library to your Gradle's build file. To do this just edit the file `MyApplication/build.gradle` and add the following line in the `dependencies` section:

```
compile files('libs/google-play-services.jar')
```

Google Maps Android API v2

Google Maps Android API allows the user of your application to explore the maps available at the Google service. The new Maps Version 2 offers more functionalities such as 3D maps, indoor and satellite maps, efficient caching and drawing using vector-based technology, and animated transitions through the map.

Let's import the sample project to examine the most important classes. Click on **File | Import Project**. Search for the sample project in your SDK installation folder and select the project root directory, `/google_play_services/samples/maps/`. In the next dialog, check the **Create project from existing sources** option. Continue clicking on **Next** in the successive dialogs and finally click on the **Finish** button and open the sample project in a new window. Now we have the Google Play Services project and the maps sample project loaded in a new window in Android Studio.

Open the `BasicMapActivity` class to examine a simple example of the use of Google Maps. You can find this activity in the maps project inside the `src/` folder. The package `com.google.android.gms.maps` contains the Google Maps Android API classes.

This activity declares a private `GoogleMap` object named as `mMap`. The **GoogleMap class** is the main class of the API and it is the entry point for all the methods related to a map. You may change the theme colors and the icons of your map to match your application style. You can also customize your map by adding markers to your maps. To add a simple marker you can use the `addMarker` method of the `GoogleMap` class. Examine the `setUpMap` method in the `BasicMapActivity` class to see the following code example:

```
mMap.addMarker(new MarkerOptions()
    .position(new LatLng(0, 0)).title("Marker"));
```

The method `addMarker` has a `MarkerOptions` object as parameter. Using the method `position` we indicate the coordinates of the marker on the map and using the method `title` we can add a custom string to show up on the marker.

To add a map into a layout we can use the `MapView` class, which extends the class `View` and displays a map. But the easiest way to place a map in an application is using a `MapFragment` object. A fragment represents a piece of the user interface or behavior that can be embedded in an activity. A fragment is a reusable module.

The **MapFragment class** wraps a view of a map to automatically handle the necessary life cycle needs of a component. It extends the class `Fragment` and can therefore be added to a layout by adding the following XML code:

```
<fragment
class="com.google.android.gms.maps.MapFragment"
android:layout_width="match_parent"
android:layout_height="match_parent" />
```

To see an example of the previous code, open the layout associated to the `BasicMapActivity` class; this is the `basic_demo.xml` file in the `/res/layout/` folder.

Finally, we need the code to obtain the `GoogleMap` object from the fragment. We can find the map `Fragment` using the method `findFragmentById`, and then we get the map from the `Fragment` using the method `getMap`.

```
mMap = ((MapFragment) getFragmentManager().
   findFragmentById(R.Id.map).getMap();
```

The example of this code in the `BasicMapActivity` class is in the `setUpMapIfNeeded` method.

One last important class is the `GoogleMapOptions` class, which defines the configuration for a map. You can also modify the initial state of a map by editing the layout XML code. Here are some interesting options available:

- `mapType`: Specify the type of a map. Its value can be `none`, `normal`, `hybrid`, `satellite`, and `terrain`.

- `uiCompass`: Define whether compass controls are enabled or disabled.

- `uiZoomControls`: Define whether zoom controls are enabled or disabled.

- `cameraTargetLat` and `cameraTargetLong`: Specify the initial camera position.

Google+ Platform for Android

Using the Google+ Platform for Android lets the developer authenticate users with the same credentials they use on Google+. You can also use the public profile and social graph to be able to welcome the users by their name, display their pictures, or connect with friends.

The package `com.google.android.gms.plus` contains the Google+ Platform for Android classes. Import the Google+ sample project to learn about the most important classes. The Google+ sample project can be found in the Google Play Services installation folder, in `/google_play_services/samples/plus/`.

- `PlusClient` and `PlusClient.Builder`: `PlusClient` is the main class of the API. It is the entry point for Google+ integration. `PlusClient.Builder` is a builder to configure the `PlusClient` object to communicate properly with the Google+ APIs.

- `PlusOneButton`: The class to implement a +1 button to recommend a URL on Google+. Add it to a layout using the following code:

```
<com.google.android.gms.plus.PlusOneButton
android:layout_width="wrap_content"
android:layout_height="wrap_content"
plus:size="standard" />
```

The available sizes are small, medium, tall, or standard.

Example code about this functionality can be found in the sample project, in the `PlusOneActivity` class in the `src/` folder and its associated layout, `plus_one_activity.xml` in the `res/layout/` folder.

- `PlusShare`: Include resources in posts shared on Google+. Example code about sharing resources can be found in the `ShareActivity` class in the `src/` folder and its associated layout, `share_activity.xml` in the `res/layout/` folder.

First of all, a `PlusClient` object should be instantiated in the `onCreate` method of your activity class to call its asynchronous method `connect`, which will connect the client to Google+ services. When the app is done using a `PlusClient` instance, it should call the method `disconnect`, which terminates the connection, and should also always be called from the `onStop` method of the activity.

Google Play In-app Billing v3

In-app Billing v3 allows you to sell virtual content from your apps. This virtual content may be paid once with a one-time billing or may be a timed concession through subscriptions or fees. Using this service, you can allow users to pay for extra features and access premium content.

Any app published in Google Play Store can implement the In-app Billing API, since it only requires the same accounts as publishing an app: a Google Play Developer Console account and a Google Wallet merchant account.

Using the Google Play Developer Console you can define your products, including type, identification code (SKU), price, description, and more. Once you have your products defined, you can access this content from this application. When the user wants to buy this content, the following purchase flow will happen between your In-app Billing application and Google Play App:

1. Your app calls `isBillingSupported()` to Google Play to check if the In-app Billing version you are using is supported.

2. If the In-app Billing API version is supported, you may use `getPurchases()` to get a list of the SKUs of the purchased items. This list will be returned in a `Bundle` object.

3. You will probably want to inform your user of the in-app purchases available. To do this your app may send a `getSkuDetails()` request, which will result in a list with the product's price, title, description, and more information available for the item.

Google Cloud Messaging

GCM for Android allows the communication between your server and your application through the use of asynchronous messages. You do not have to worry about handling low-level aspects of this communication such as queuing and message construction. Using this service, you can easily implement a notification system for your application.

You have two options when using GCM:

- The server can inform your app that there is new data available to be fetched from the server and then the application gets this data.

- The server can send the data directly in a message. The message payload can be up to 4 KB. This allows your application to access the data at once and act accordingly.

In order to send or receive messages, you will need to get a registration ID. This registration ID identifies the combination of device and application. To allow your app to use the GCM service, you need to add the following line to the manifest file of your project:

```
<uses-permission android:name="com.google.
  android.c2dm.permission.RECEIVE"/>
```

The main class you will need to use is `GoogleCloudMessaging`. This class is available in the package `com.google.android.gms.gcm`.

Summary

By the end of this chapter, we know about the available Google Play Services. We learned how to improve our application using Google Play Services through its client library and Android package. The reader should have successfully installed the Google Play Services client library in Android Studio using the SDK Manager and should be able to build applications using the library features. We have also learned some tips about Google Maps v2, Google+ Platform for Android authentication, Google Play In-app Billing, and GCM.

In the next chapter we will learn about some useful tools available in the Android Studio. We will again use the SDK Manager in detail to install different packages. We will also learn about the AVD Manager to be able to have different virtual devices to test our applications on. We will generate Javadoc documentation for our project using the Javadoc utility and we will learn about the version control systems available in Android Studio.

7
Tools

In the previous chapter we've learned about useful services that Google provides which can be used by developers to improve their applications. Now, we will learn about tools available in Android Studio that make our life easier as developers. Have you wondered how to manage the Android platforms? Do you want to have your project clearly documented? Are you working as a group of developers and need a version control manager integrated with Android Studio?

This chapter shows the most important additional tools provided in Android Studio: Android SDK tools, Javadoc, and version control integration. First, we will learn about the Software Development Kit Manager available in Android Studio from which we'll be able to examine, update, and install different components for our project. Next, we will review the Android Virtual Device Manager, where we can edit the virtual devices in which we will be testing our project. We will also learn about how to have a complete documentation using the Javadoc tool, and how to have version control using the systems available in Android Studio.

These are the topics we'll be covering in this chapter:

- SDK Manager
- AVD Manager
- Javadoc
- Version control

Software Development Kit Manager

The **Software Development Kit (SDK) Manager** is an Android tool integrated in Android Studio to control our Android SDK installation. From this tool we can examine the Android platforms installed in our system, update them, install new platforms, or install some other components such as Google Play Services or the Android Support Library.

To open the SDK Manager from Android Studio, navigate to the menu **Tools |
Android | SDK Manager**. You can also click on the shortcut from the toolbar. On the
top of the manager the SDK path that was configured in Android Studio is displayed.

The SDK Manager displays the list of the available packages with the following
properties:

- **Name**: Name of the package or the container that aggregates some
  related packages.
- **API**: API number in which the package was added.
- **Rev**: Number of the package revision or version.
- **Status**: Status of the package regarding your system. The status can be **Not
  installed**, **Installed**, **Update available**, **Not compatible**, or **Obsolete**.

The packages can be filtered by their state using the checkboxes under the list and
they can be sorted by the API level or by the repository they are downloaded to.
These options are also accessible from the top menu **Packages**.

From the menu **Tools | Manage Add-on Sites** we can examine the list of the official
sites that provide the add-ons and extra packages. In the **User Defined Sites** menu
we can add our custom external sites.

Next to the name of the packages there is a checkbox to select the packages we want to
install, update, or delete. As shown in the following screenshot, the packages that are
installed in our system but have updates available are checked by default. If there is a
new Android platform version that is not installed, its packages will also be checked.

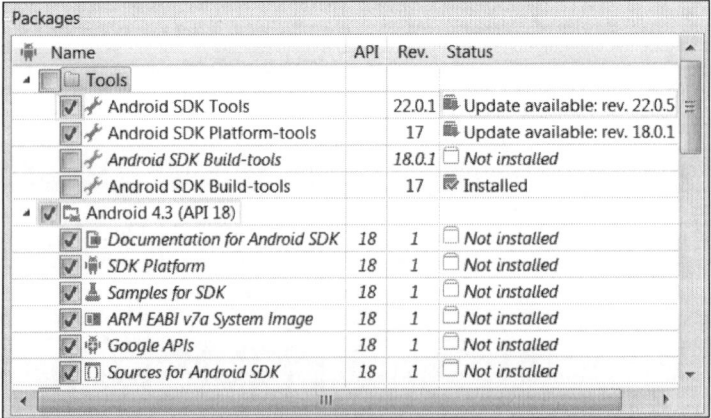

The total number of selected packages to be installed or updated is indicated in the
text of the button on the bottom of the dialog. The button under it indicates the total
number of selected packages to be deleted.

Check the packages that need to be updated, check the last Android platform if you do not have it installed, and check the minimum platform supported by our application, Android 2.3.3 (API 10), to be able to test our application in a virtual device using this version. Click on the **Install** button.

In the next dialog, we have to accept the package licenses. Check the **Accept License** radio button and click on the **Install** button. The installation or updating of the packages will start showing its progress. Firstly, the manager downloads the packages, then unzips them, and finally installs them.

Remember to check the SDK Manager from time to time to check for updates.

Android Virtual Device Manager

The **Android Virtual Device Manager** (**AVD Manager**) is an Android tool integrated in Android Studio to manage the Android virtual devices that will be executed in the Android emulator.

To open the AVD Manager from Android Studio, navigate to the menu **Tools | Android | AVD Manager**. You can also click on the shortcut from the toolbar. The AVD Manager displays the list of the existing virtual devices in the default tab **Android Virtual Devices**. Since we have not created any virtual device, initially the list should be empty. To create our first virtual device, click on the **New** button to open the configuration dialog:

- **AVD Name**: Name of the virtual device.
- **Device**: Select one of the available device configurations. These configurations are the ones we tested in the layout editor preview. Select the Nexus 4 device to load its parameters in the dialog.
- **Target**: Select the device Android platform. We have to create one virtual device with the minimum platform supported by our application and another virtual device with the target platform of our application. Both of these platforms were configured when we created the project. For this first virtual device, select the target platform, Android 4.2.2 (API 17).

- **CPU/ABI**: Select the device architecture. The value of this field is set when we select the target platform. Each platform has its architecture, so if we do not have it installed, the following message will be shown: **No system images installed for this target**. To solve this, open the SDK Manager and search for one of the architectures of the target platform, ARM EABI v7a System Image or Intel x86 Atom System Image.

- **Keyboard**: Select if a hardware keyboard is displayed in the emulator. Check it.

- **Skin**: Select if additional hardware controls are displayed in the emulator. Check it.

- **Front Camera**: Select if the emulator has a front camera. The camera can be emulated or can be real by the use of a webcam from the computer. Select **None**.

- **Back Camera**: Select if the emulator has a back camera. Select **None**.

- **Memory Options**: Select the memory parameters of the virtual device. Keep the default values, unless a warning message is shown; in this case, follow the instructions of the message. For example, select 256 for the **RAM** memory and 64 for the **VM Heap**.

- **Internal Storage**: Select the virtual device storage size, for example: 200 MiB.

- **SD Card**: Select the size of the SD card or select a file to behave as the SD card. This parameter is optional.

- **Emulation Options**: The **Snapshot** option saves the state of the emulator in order to load faster the next time. Check it. The **Use Host GPU** option tries to accelerate the GPU hardware to run the emulator faster.

Give the virtual device a meaningful name to easily recognize it, like AVD_nexus4_api17. Click on the **OK** button.

The new virtual device is now listed in the AVD Manager with a green tick icon indicating that it is valid. These icons indicate the state of the virtual device: if it is valid, if it failed to load, or if its state is repairable. The icon legend is explained on the bottom of the manager window. Select the recently created virtual device to enable the remaining actions:

- **Edit**: Edit the virtual device configuration.

- **Delete**: Delete the virtual device.

- **Repair**: Option available if the virtual device failed to load but it can be repaired. This action tries to repair the error state of the virtual device.

- **Details**: Open a dialog detailing the virtual device characteristics.

- **Start**: Run the virtual device.

Click on the **Start** button to open the launch dialog. Check the options relative to the snapshot and click on the **Launch** button. The emulator will be opened as shown in the following screenshot. Wait until it is completely loaded and then you will be able to try it.

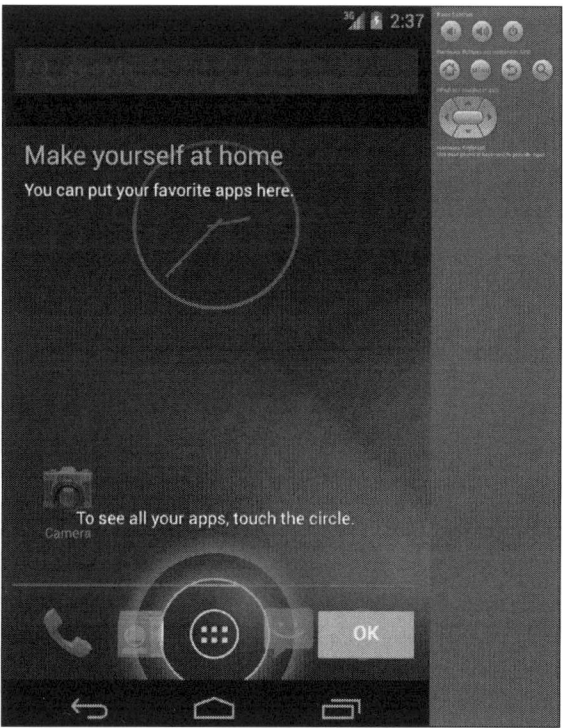

From the AVD Manager we can also configure the device definitions. The device definitions are used in the layout preview and are the base of the virtual devices. Open the **Device Definitions** tab where the existing definitions are listed. We can create a new device definition using the **New Device** button, we can clone an existing device to create a new one easily using the **Clone** button, we can delete them using the **Delete** button, or we can create a virtual device based on the device definition using the **Create AVD** button.

Click on the **New Device** button to examine the existing configuration parameters. The most important parameters that define a device are:

- **Name**: Name of the device.

- **Screen Size (in)**: Screen size in inches. This value determines the size category of the device. Type a value of 4.0 and notice how the **Size** value (on the right side) is **normal**. Now type a value of 7.0 and the **Size** field changes its value to **large**. This parameter along with the screen resolution also determines the density category.

- **Resolution (px)**: Screen resolution in pixels. This value determines the density category of the device. With a screen size of 4.0 inches, type a value of 768 x 1280 and notice how the density value is **xhdpi**. Change the screen size to 6.0 inches and the density value changes to **hdpi**. Now change the resolution to 480 x 800 and the density value is **mdpi**.

- **Sensors**: Sensors available in the device: accelerometer, GPS, gyroscope, or proximity sensor.

- **RAM**: RAM memory size of the device.

- **Buttons**: Indicate if the home, back, or menu buttons of the device are available via software or hardware.

- **Device States**: Check the allowed states.

Create a new device with a screen size of 4.7 inches, a resolution of 800 x 1280, a RAM value of 200 MiB, software buttons enabled, and both portrait and landscape states enabled. Name it as My Device. Click on the **Create Device** button.

The AVD Manager now displays in the device list our device definition. Also, in Android Studio, open the main layout with the graphical editor and click on the list of the devices. As the next screenshot shows, our custom device definition appears and we can select it to preview the layout:

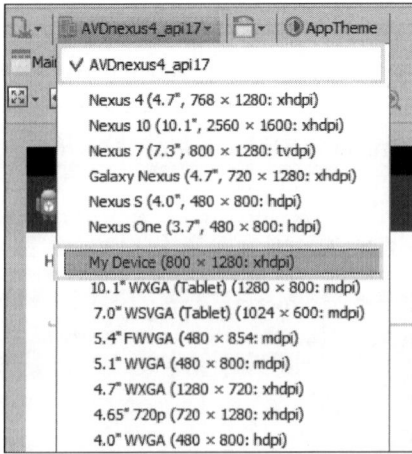

Generating Javadoc

Javadoc is a utility to document Java code in HTML format. The Javadoc documentation is generated from comments and tags added to the Java classes or methods. The comments start with the /** string and end with */. Inside these comments, some tags can be added such as @param to describe a method parameter, @throws to describe an exception that can be thrown by the method, or @version to indicate the version of the class or method.

The use of Javadoc is integrated in Android Studio. We can use code completion when typing the Javadoc comments and the documentation will appear in the pop-up tool tips of the code elements.

To generate a complete Javadoc, we have to write the Javadoc comments about our classes and methods. Open the main activity of our project to add the Javadoc comments to the method onAcceptClick we created in *Chapter 5, Creating User Interfaces*. Place the caret on the line before the method declaration, type /**, and press *Enter*. The Javadoc comments are automatically inserted containing the available information from the method declaration: parameters and return type. In this case, there is no return type.

The first line of the documentation comments is the method description. Then, explain each parameter and the return type. The method should now look like this:

```
/**
 * Method executed when the user clicks on the Accept button.
 * Change the greeting message to include the name introduced by the
user in the editText box.
 *
 * @param v View the user clicked
 */
public void onAcceptClick(View v) { ... }
```

This information about the method will now be displayed as its documentation in the emerging dialogs. The following screenshot shows the dialog that should appear over the method:

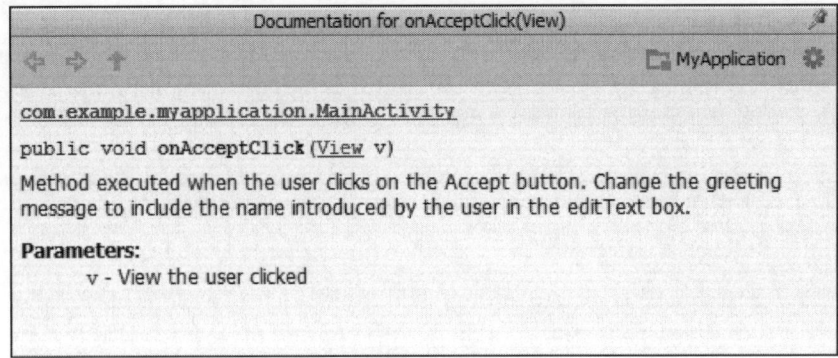

To generate the Javadoc documentation, navigate on the top menu to **Tools** | **Generate Javadoc**. A dialog showing the Javadoc options will be opened. We can choose the scope, the output directory, the visibility of the included elements, or if we want to create a hierarchy tree, a navigation bar, and an index.

Check **Current File** as scope to generate just the documentation of our main activity. Select an output directory from your system. Reduce the visibility to public and click on the **OK** button. The Javadoc documentation in HTML format has been created in the output directory, the `index.html` file being the start point. Navigate through the documentation to open the `MainActivity` class. Notice that the `onCreate` method whose visibility is protected does not appear due to the fact that we reduced the visibility of the generated Javadoc to public elements.

Version control system

Android Studio integrates some version control systems: Git, Mercurial, or Subversion. To enable the version control integration navigate on the top menu to **VCS** | **Enable Version Control Integration** and select the type of system. Now some more options have been added to the **VCS** menu.

The first step is to do the checkout from the version control system. Navigate to **VCS** | **Checkout from Version Control**, click on the add icon, and type the repository URL:

- To update the entire project navigate to the option **VCS** | **Update Project**
- To commit all the changes of the project navigate to the option **VCS** | **Commit Changes**
- To clean up the project navigate to the option **VCS** | **Cleanup Project**

The version control actions can also be applied to individual files. Click on any file of the project using the right mouse button and select the **Subversion** section. From the emerging menu we can add the file to the repository, add it to the ignore list, browse the changes, revert the changes, or lock it.

A simpler way to control the file versions is using the local history. Open the main activity file in the editor and navigate to **VCS | Local History | Show History**. The file history dialog will be opened. On the left side of the dialog, the available versions of the file are listed. Select an older version to compare it to the current version of the file. The differences between the older version and the current version are highlighted. A gray color is used to indicate a block of deleted code, a blue color to highlight the text that has changed, and a green color to indicate the new inserted text. From the top icons we can revert the changes and configure the whitespaces visualization. The next screenshot shows the comparison between two versions of our main activity. We can observe how the method we recently added, the onAcceptClick method, is highlighted in green.

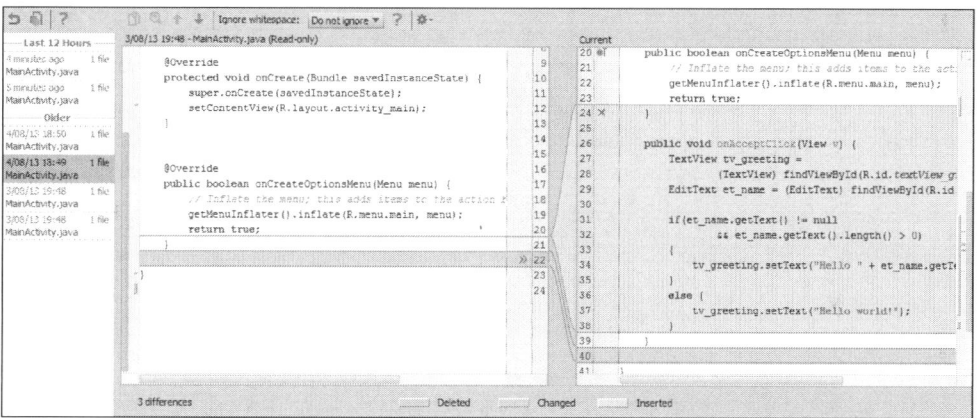

We can also examine the local history of just a specific block of code. Close the dialog, select some lines of code from the editor, and navigate to **VCS | Local History | Show History for Selection**. The same history dialog will be opened, but this time it displays the versions of the selected code.

Summary

By the end of this chapter we should have the knowledge to use the Android SDK Manager tool to install, update, or examine available platforms for our project. We should be able to create a new Android Virtual Device and to edit it whenever it is deemed necessary. Creating a complete documentation of our project should no longer be a problem using Javadoc, and we should also be able to work with a version control system integrated in Android Studio.

In the next chapter we will keep on working with Android Studio integrated features. In this case we will be learning about the emulation of our project and how to debug it. We will learn about the debugger, the console, or the LogCat tool. We will also learn about more advanced debugging tools such as the Dalvik Debug Monitor Server (DDMS). We will study in depth about this monitor server, going through each of its available utilities.

8
Debugging

The debugging environment is one of the most important features of an IDE. Using a debugging tool allows you to easily optimize your application and improve its performance. Do you want to use one of these debug tools while programming in Android Studio? Android Studio includes the **Dalvik Debug Monitor Server (DDMS)** debugging tool.

In this chapter we will start by learning about the run and debug options and how to emulate our application in one of the Android virtual devices we learned to create in the previous chapter. We will learn about the debugger tab, the console tab, and the LogCat tab in depth. We will also learn how to use breakpoints using the debugger and how to run our application stopping in those breakpoints. We will end this chapter with information about each tab available in the advanced debugging tool included in Android Studio DDMS.

These are the topics we'll be covering in this chapter:

* Debugging
* LogCat
* DDMS tools

Running and debugging

Android applications can be run from Android Studio in a real device using the USB connection or in a virtual device using the emulator. Virtual devices make it possible to test our applications in different types of hardware and software configurations. In this chapter we are using the emulator to run and debug our application because of its simplicity and flexibility.

To directly run an application, navigate to the menu **Run | Run 'MyApplication'**. You can also click on the play icon button from the toolbar. To debug an application, navigate to the menu **Run | Debug 'MyApplication'** or click on the bug icon from the toolbar.

When we select the debug option, a dialog to choose the device is opened. The first option is to choose a running device; the available connected devices are listed, real or virtual ones. The second option is to launch a new instance of the emulator; the available virtual devices are listed. Check the **Launch emulator** option and select the virtual device created in *Chapter 7, Tools*. Click on **OK**. The emulator will be launched. The next time we run or debug the application, the emulator is already running, so we will choose the first option (**Choose a running device**).

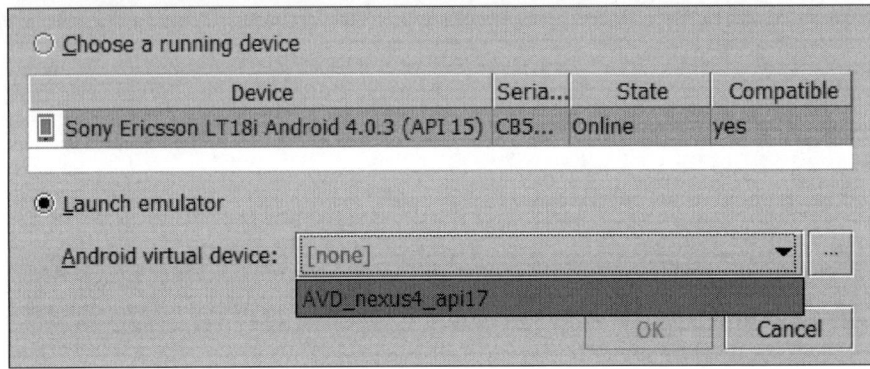

While debugging, on the bottom of Android Studio there are three tabs: **Debugger**, **Console**, and **LogCat**.

The **Console** displays the events that are taking place while the emulator is being launched. Open it to examine the messages and check that the emulator and the application are correctly being executed. The actions that should appear are:

- `Waiting for device`: Start point when the emulator is being launched.
- `Uploading file`: The application is packed and stored in the device.
- `Installing`: The application is being installed in the device. After the installation a success message should be printed.
- `Launching application`: The application starts to execute.
- `Waiting for process`: The application should now be running and the debug system tries to connect to the application process in the device.

After the success of the previous steps, the application will be visible in the emulator. Test it by typing any name in the text input and click on the **Accept** button. The greeting message should change.

The **Debugger** manages the breakpoints, controls the execution of the code, and shows information about the variables. To add a breakpoint in our code, just click on the left edge of a line code. A red point will appear next to the line code to indicate the breakpoint. To delete the breakpoint, click on it. If you click on a breakpoint using the right mouse button, more options are available. We can disable it without deleting it or we can set a condition for the breakpoint.

Add a breakpoint in the conditional statement of the `onAcceptClick` method of our main activity and debug the application again.

```java
MainActivity.java ×
34
35        public void onAcceptClick(View v) {
36            TextView tv_greeting = (TextView) findViewById(R.id.textView_greeting);
37            EditText et_name = (EditText) findViewById(R.id.editText_name);
38
39            if( et_name.getText().length() > 0) {
40                tv_greeting.setText("Hello " + et_name.getText());
41            }
42        }
43    }
44
```

Enter your name in the application and click on the **Accept** button. When the execution gets to the breakpoint, it pauses and the debugger tab is opened. Since we added the breakpoint in the conditional statement, before assigning the text, our greeting message has not changed.

From the debugger tab we can examine the method call hierarchy and the variables state at that point of execution. The available variables are the parameter of the method (v), the `TextView` and `EditText` objects obtained by the `findViewById` method and the reference to the current activity (`this`). Expand the `EditText` object named as `et_name` and search for the property `mText`. This property should contain the name you typed before:

- To execute the next line of code without stepping into the method call, navigate to **Run | Step Over** or use the keyboard shortcut indicated for this option, usually key *F8*

- To step into the method call, navigate to **Run | Step Into** or press *F7*

- To resume the execution until the next breakpoint if there is one, navigate to **Run | Resume Program** or press *F9*

- To stop the execution, navigate to **Run | Stop** or press *Ctrl + F2*

These options, among others, are also available from the debugger tab as icon shortcuts.

Expand the `tv_greeting` object to check the value of its `mText` property. Now step over the conditional statement and step over the call of the `setText` method. Notice how the value of the `mText` property has changed. Finally, resume the execution so the greeting message changes in the device screen.

LogCat

LogCat is the Android logging system that displays all the log messages generated by the Android system in the running device. Log messages have several levels of significance. From the LogCat tab we can filter the log messages by these levels. For example, if we select the information level as filter, the messages from information, warning, and error levels will be displayed.

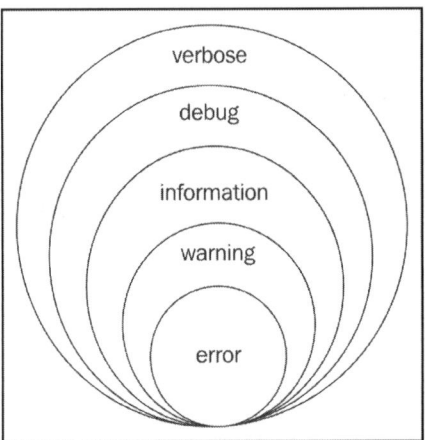

To print log messages from our code we need to import the `Log` class. This class has a method for each level: v method for debug level, d method for verbose, i method for information, w method for warning, and e method for error messages. These methods receive two string parameters. The first string parameter usually identifies the source class of the message and the second string parameter identifies the message itself. To identify the source class, we recommend using a constant static string tag, although in the next example we directly use the string to simplify the code. Add the following log messages in the `onAcceptClick` method of our main activity:

```
if(et_name.getText().length() > 0) {
  Log.i("MainActivity", "Name read: " + et_name.getText());
  tv_greeting.setText("Hello " + et_name.getText());
}
```

```
else {
  Log.w("MainActivity", "No name typed, greeting didn't change");
}
```

We have a log message to inform about the name obtained from the user input and a log message to print a warning if the user did not type any name. Remove any breakpoint we previously created and then debug the application.

The LogCat tab has printed all the log messages generated by the device, so reading the messages of our application can be complex. We need to filter the messages. In the LogCat tab there is an expandable list with the **No Filters** option selected. Expand it and select the option **Edit Filter Configuration**. A dialog to create filters is opened. Log messages can be filtered by their tag or their content using regular expressions, by the name of the package that printed them, by the process ID (PID), or by their level.

Create a new filter named `MyApplication` and filter by **Package Name** using the package of our application as value: `com.example.myapplication`. Click on **OK**. Now the LogCat log has been filtered and it is easier to read our messages.

1. Focus the emulator window, enter a name in the application, and click on **Accept**. Observe how our log message is printed in the LogCat view.

2. Delete your name in the application and click on **Accept**. This time, the warning message is printed. Notice the different colors used for each type of message.

If we double-click on a LogCat entrance, we can navigate to the source line that generated that log message.

DDMS

The Dalvik Debug Monitor Server (DDMS) is a more advanced debugging tool from the SDK that has also been integrated into Android Studio. This tool is able to monitor both a real device and the emulator.

To open the DDMS perspective navigate to **Tools | Android | Monitor (DDMS included)**. You can also click on the Android icon button from the toolbar. A new window will be opened with the DDMS perspective.

On the left part of the window, the list of connected devices is shown. Currently, just our virtual device is listed. In the devices section the list of the processes running on each device is also presented. We should be able to locate our application in the processes of the device we launched before. From the toolbar of the devices section, we can stop a process using the stop sign icon button. We can also take a screen capture of the virtual device by clicking on the camera icon button. Some of the other options will be explained later.

On the right part of the window, detailed information of the device is provided. This information is divided into seven tabs: **Threads**, **Heap**, **Allocation Tracker**, **Network Statistics**, **File Explorer**, **Emulator Control**, and **System Information**. On the bottom part of the window is the LogCat, which has been also integrated in the DDMS perspective.

Threads

The threads tab displays the list of threads that belong to the selected process. Select our application process from the devices section. The process is identified by the package name com.example.myapplication. Click on the **Update Threads** icon button from the toolbar of the devices section and the threads will be loaded in the content of the tab.

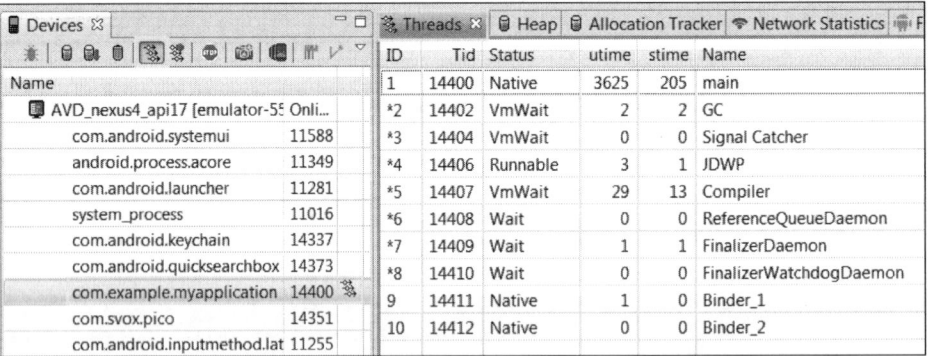

The first columns are the IDs of the threads. The **Status** column indicates the thread state, **utime** indicates the total time spent by the thread executing user code, **stime** indicates the total time spent by the thread executing system code, and **Name** indicates the name of the thread. The threads that interest us are those that spend time executing our user code.

This tool is useful if we create threads in our application apart from the main thread. We can check if they are being executed at a certain point of the application or if their execution time is moderate or not.

Method profiling

Method profiling is a tool to measure the performance of the methods' execution in the selected process. The measured parameters are the number of calls and the CPU time spent while executing. There are two types of spent time, the exclusive and the inclusive:

- **Exclusive time**: Time spent in the execution of the method itself.

- **Inclusive time**: Total time spent in the execution of the method. This measure includes the time spent by any called methods inside the method. These called functions are known as its children methods.

To collect the method profiling data, select our application process from the devices section and click on the **Start Method Profiling** icon button from the toolbar of the devices section, next to the **Update Threads** icon button. Then perform some actions in the application, for example, in our example application, type a name and click on the **Accept** button in order to execute the onAcceptClick method of the main activity. Stop the method profiling by clicking on the **Stop Method Profiling** icon button.

When the method profiling is stopped, a new tab with the resultant trace is opened in the DDMS perspective. On the top of this new tab, the method calls are represented in a time graph; each row belongs to a thread. On the bottom of the trace, the summary of the time spent in a method is represented in a table.

Order the methods by their name to search for our onAcceptClick method. Click on it to expand the detailed information about the execution of this method. Notice the following facts:

- The children methods called inside the onAcceptClick method are listed. We can see the EditText.getText method, the Activity.findViewById method, or the TextView.setText method, which indeed we directly call inside the method in the following screenshot.

- The number of calls. For example, we can see that the Activity. findViewById method is called twice: that is one call to find the TextView object and a second call to find the EditText object.

- The exclusive time columns have no value for the parents or children methods due to their own definition of this type of measured time.

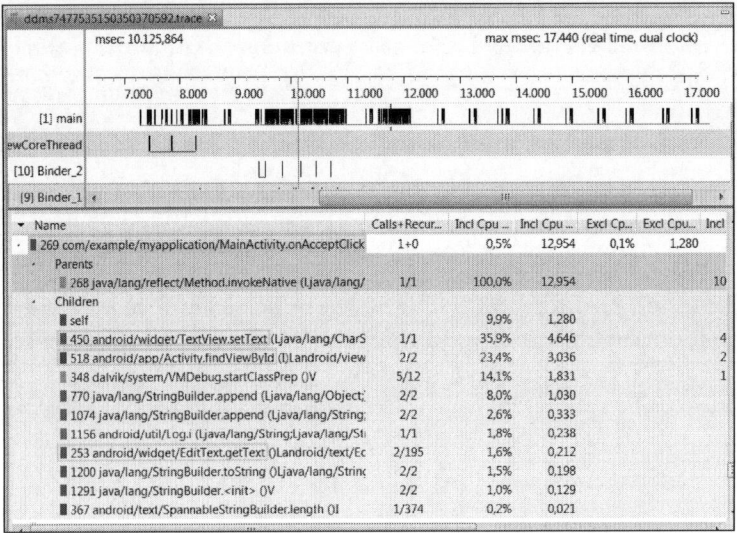

Method profiling is very useful to detect methods that spend too much time in its execution and be able to optimize them. We can learn which are the most expensive methods, to avoid unnecessary calls to them.

Heap

The heap tab displays the heap memory usage information and statistics of the selected process. Select the application process and click on the **Update Heap** icon button from the toolbar of the devices section to enable it. The heap information is shown after a garbage collector (GC) execution. To force it, click on the **Cause GC** button or click on the garbage icon button from the toolbar of the devices section.

The first table displays the summary of the heap usage: the total size, the allocated space, the free space, and the number of allocated objects. The statistics table gives the details of the objects allocated in the heap by its type: the number of objects, the total size of those objects, the size of the smallest and largest objects, the median size, and the average size. Select one of the types to load the bottom bar graph. The graph draws the number of the objects of that type by its size in bytes. If we click on the graph using the right mouse button, we can change its properties (title, colors, font, labels...) and save it as an image in PNG format.

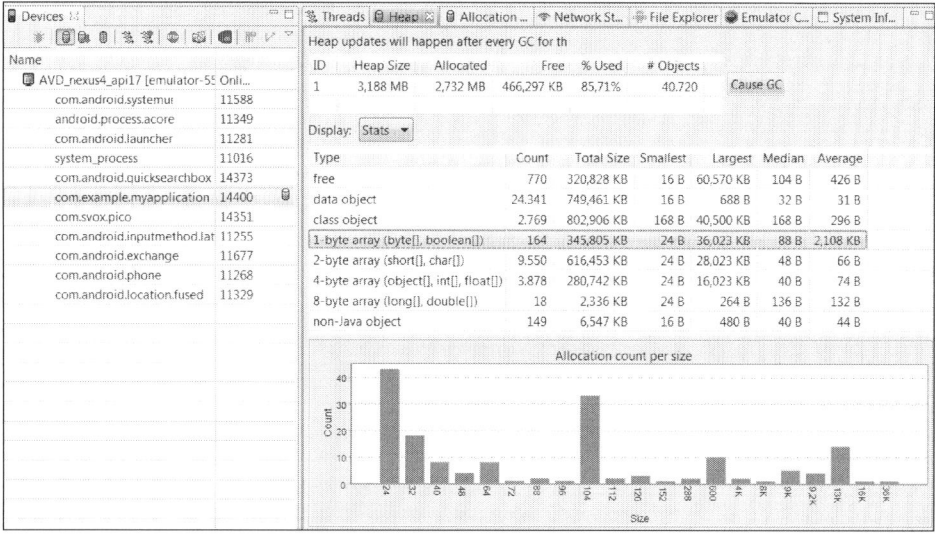

Allocation tracker

The allocation tracker tab displays the memory allocations of the selected process. Select the application process and click on the **Start Tracking** button to start tracking the memory information. Then click on the **Get Allocations** button to get the list of allocated objects.

We can use the filter on the top of the tab to filter the objects allocated in our own classes. Type our package name in the filter, com.example.myapplication. For each object, the table shows its allocation size, the thread, the object or class, and the method in which the object was allocated. Click on any object to see more information, for example, the line number that allocated it. Finally, click on the **Stop Tracking** button.

The allocation tracker is very useful to examine the objects that are being allocated when doing certain interactions in our application in order to improve the memory consumption.

Network statistics

The network statistics tab displays how our application uses the network resources. To get the network statistics of any application that uses the network, click on the **Start** button. The data transfers will start to appear in the graph.

The network statistics are useful to optimize the network requests in our code and control the data transferred at a certain point of the execution.

File Explorer

This tab exposes the whole filesystem of the device. For each element we can examine its size, date, or permissions. Navigate to /data/app/ to search for our application package file, com.example.myapplication.apk.

Emulator control

Emulator control allows us to emulate some special states or activities in the virtual device. We can test our application in different environments and situations to check that it behaves as expected. If our application has features that depend on the device physical location, we can use mock locations:

- **Telephony Status**: Choose the voice and data status, its speed, and latency
- **Telephony Actions**: Simulate an incoming call or SMS
- **Location Controls**: Set the geolocation of the device

System information

The system information tab presents the frame render time, the total CPU load, and the total memory usage of the device as graphs. We can search for our application and easily compare it along with the rest of the processes running on the device.

We can change the properties of the graphs such as colors, font, title and we can save them as images in the PNG format. To open these options, click on the graph elements using the right mouse button.

Open the CPU load and save the graph when our application is running in the foreground. Then close the application and update the CPU load by clicking on the **Update from Device** button. Notice the difference between both graphs and notice the growth of the idle percentage.

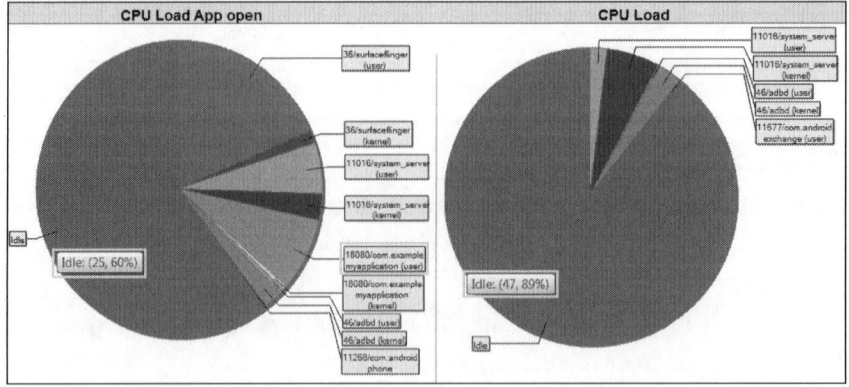

Summary

By the end of this chapter, the users should know the different launch options for their application and how to use the console and the LogCat for debugging. They should also have learned how to debug an application and to interpret the data provided by the DDMS in each of the tabs available.

In the next chapter we will prepare our application for its release using Android Studio. First we will learn about the necessary steps to prepare our application before building it in the release mode. We will learn about how the applications are compressed in APK files and how to generate our own APK. Finally, we will learn how to get our certificate as developers and how to generate a signed APK file, making it ready for release.

9
Preparing for Release

In the previous chapter you've learned enough to test and debug your application. What do you need to prepare your application for release? How can you do this using Android Studio?

This chapter describes the necessary steps to prepare your application for release using Android Studio. First of all we will learn about the Application Packages files, a variation of the JAR files in which Android applications are packed. We will then learn how we need to change our application after fully testing it. Finally, we will sign our application APK (**Application Package**) file, leaving it ready to upload to any market such as Google Play.

These are the topics we'll be covering in this chapter:

- Preparing for release
- APK files
- Getting a certificate
- Generating a signed APK

What is an APK file

Android applications are packed in a file with the `.APK` extension, which is a variation of a Java JAR (**Java Archive**) file. These files are just compressed ZIP files, so their content can be easily explored. An APK file usually contains:

- `assets/`: A folder that contains the assets files of the application. This is the same `assets` folder existing in the project.
- `META-INF/`: A folder that contains our certificates.
- `lib/`: A folder that contains compiled code if necessary for a processor.
- `res/`: A folder that contains the application resources.

- `AndroidManifest.xml`: The application manifest file.
- `classes.dex`: A file that contains the application compiled code.
- `resources.arsc`: A file that contains some precompiled resources.

With the `APK` file, the application can be distributed and installed on the Android operating system. Android applications can be distributed as you prefer, through app markets such as Google Play, Amazon Appstore, or Opera Mobile Store; through your own website; or even through an e-mail to your users. If you choose any of the last two options, take into account that Android by default blocks installations from locations different from Google Play. You should inform your users that they need to disable this restriction in their devices to be able to install your application. They have to check the **Unknown sources** option from the **Settings | Security** menu of their Android devices.

Applications have to be signed with a private key when they are built. An application can't be installed in a device or even in the emulator if it is not signed. To build our application there are two modes, debug and release. Both `APK` versions contain the same folders and compiled files. The difference is the key used to sign them:

- **Debug**: When we run and tested our application in the previous chapters, we were in the debug mode, but we didn't have any key nor did anything to sign our application. The Android SDK tools automatically create a debug key, an alias, and their passwords to sign the `APK`. This process occurs when we are running or debugging our application with Android Studio without us realizing that. We can't publish an `APK` signed with the debug key created by the SDK tools.

- **Release**: We have to build a release version when we want to distribute our application in order to be able to install it in other Android devices. It is a requirement that the APK file is signed with a certificate for which the developer keeps the private key. In this case, we need our own private key, alias, and password and provide them to the build tools. The certificate identifies the developer of the application and can be a self-signed certificate. It is not necessary for a certificate authority to sign the certificate.

> Keep the key store with your certificate in a secure place. To upgrade your application you have to use the same key in order to upload the new version. If you lose the key store, you won't be able to update your application. You will have to create a new application with a different package name.

Previous steps

Before we generate the APK file, it is necessary to prepare our application for building it in the release mode.

Firstly, make sure you have completely tested your application. We recommend testing your application:

- On a device using the minimum required platform
- On a device using the target platform
- On a device using the latest available platform
- On a real device and not just in the emulator
- On a variety of screen resolutions and sizes
- On a tablet if your application supports them
- Switching to the landscape mode if you allow it, both in a mobile device and in a tablet
- On different network conditions, such as no Internet connectivity or low coverage
- If your application uses the GPS or any location service, test it when they are not activated in the device
- Behavior of the back button

Secondly, we have to check the log messages that are printed from our application. Printing some log messages can be considered a security vulnerability. Logs generated by the Android system can be captured and analyzed, so we should avoid showing critical information about the application's internal working. You should also remove the `android:debuggable` property from the application manifest file. You can also set this property to `false`.

Thirdly, if your application communicates with a server, check that the configured URL is the production one. It is possible that during the debug phase, you referenced to a URL of a server in a pre-release environment.

Finally, set the correct value for the `android:versionCode` and `android:versionName` properties from the application manifest file. The version code is a number (integer) that represents the application version. New versions should have greater version codes. This code is used to determine if an application installed in a device is the last version, or there is a newer one.

The version name is a string that represents the application version. Unlike the version code, the version name is visible to the user and appears in the public information about the application. It is just an informative version name to the user and is not used for any internal purpose.

Specify a value of 1 for the version code and 1.0 for the version name. The manifest tag should look like:

```
<manifest xmlns:android="http://schemas.android.com/apk/res/android"
    package="com.example.myapplication"
    android:versionCode="1"
    android:versionName="1.0" >
```

A new version of our application will have a value of 2 for the version code and, for example, 1.1 for the version name.

```
<manifest xmlns:android="http://schemas.android.com/apk/res/android"
    package="com.example.myapplication"
    android:versionCode="2"
    android:versionName="1.1" >
```

Generating a signed APK

To generate the signed APK, navigate on the menu **Build | Generate Signed APK**. In the dialog to generate the signed APK, we are asked for a certificate. The APK is signed by this certificate and it indicates that it belongs to us.

If it is our first application, probably we do not have any certificate. Click on the **Create new** button to open the dialog box to create a new key store. We have to fill in the following information.

- **Key store path**: Path in your system to create the key store. The key store is a file with a .jks extension. For example, name it as release_keystore.jks.
- **Password**: Key store password. You have to confirm it.
- **Alias**: Alias for your certificate and pair of public and private key. For example, name it as releasekey.
- **Password**: Certificate password. You have to confirm it.
- **Validity**: The certificate will be valid until the validity date. A value of 25 years or more is recommended.
- **Certificate**: Personal information contained in the certificate. Type your first and last name, organizational unit, organization, city or locality, state or province, and country code. For example, AS example as **Organizational Unit**, packtpub as **Organization**, and ES as **Country Code**.

Click on **OK**. The dialog box to create the signed APK is now loaded with the key store data. The next time we create a signed APK, we already have a certificate and therefore we will click on the **Choose existing** button. Click on the **Next** button. In the next step, select the path to save the APK file and click **Finish**. When the APK is completely generated, we will be informed as can be seen from the following screenshot:

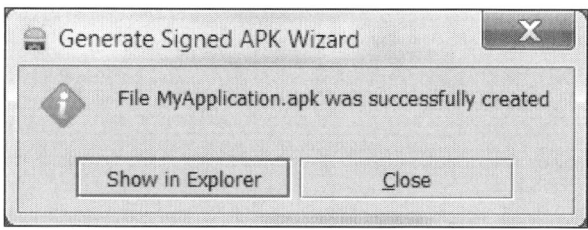

We should have the APK file created in the selected path. Click on the **Show in Explorer** button to open the folder containing the generated package, or click on the **Close** button to just close the message.

Now that we have the release APK file, it is recommended to test it again in a device before distributing it.

Summary

We have learned how to make an APK file and how to modify our application to make it ready for release. We have also learned how to sign our application using our developer certificate. By the end of this chapter, the user should have generated a signed APK prepared for its release.

In the next chapter we will learn about how to get help using Android Studio. We will access Android Studio online documentation and go through the help topics. Finally, we will learn about keeping our Android Studio instance updated using the built-in feature for it.

10
Getting Help

While developing applications in a new IDE there will always be doubts on how to do a certain action. A successful IDE usually includes help wizards and documentation that help users with different problems. Are you wondering how to get help using Android Studio?

In this last chapter we will learn about the Android Studio documentation and help topics. We will learn the topics available in the official documentation that can be accessed online on the official Android website. Finally, we will learn about how to keep our Android Studio instance up-to-date using the update functionality.

Topics covered:

- Android Studio help
- Online documentation
- Android Studio updates

Getting help from Android Studio

Android Studio documentation is included in the IntelliJ IDEA web help. This documentation is accessible from Android Studio in the menu **Help | Online Documentation**, or at `http://www.jetbrains.com/idea/documentation/`. A better option is to navigate to **Help | Help Topics** to directly open the documentation contents tree, or at `http://www.jetbrains.com/idea/webhelp/intellij-idea.html`. There are also some online video tutorials available. Navigate to **Help | JetBrains TV** or open the URL `http://tv.jetbrains.net/`.

To quickly find actions of Android Studio, we can use the **Help | Find Action** option. Type the action you are looking for and the list of matching actions will be displayed.

Finally, Android Studio provides the tip of the day functionality. The tip of the day explains in a dialog box a trick about Android Studio. Every time you open Android Studio, this dialog box is shown. We can navigate through more tips using the **Previous Tip** and **Next Tip** buttons. By deselecting the **Show Tips on Startup** checkbox, we can disable this functionality. The tip dialog box can be opened by navigating to **Help | Tip of the Day**.

Android online documentation

The official Android documentation provided by Google is available at `http://developer.android.com/`. This documentation contains all the necessary guides to learn not only how to program Android applications but also how to design for Android and how to distribute and promote our applications. Since this website is quite extensive, here we are listing some of the specific guides useful to increase the knowledge exposed in the chapters of this book.

1. *Chapter 1, Installing and Configuring Android Studio*:

    ◦   Getting Started with Android Studio, at `http://developer.android.com/sdk/installing/studio.html`

    ◦   Troubleshooting, at `http://developer.android.com/sdk/installing/studio.html#Troubleshooting`

    ◦   Known issues, at `http://tools.android.com/knownissues`

2. *Chapter 2, Starting a Project*:

    ◦   Iconography | Launcher, at `http://developer.android.com/design/style/iconography.html#launcher`

    ◦   Using Code Templates, at `http://developer.android.com/tools/projects/templates.html`

3. *Chapter 3, Navigating a Project*:

    ◦   Managing Projects, at `http://developer.android.com/tools/projects/`

    ◦   Android Studio Tips and Tricks | Project Structure, at `http://developer.android.com/sdk/installing/studio-tips.html#Project`

4. *Chapter 4, Using the Code Editor*:

    ◦   Android Studio Tips and Tricks | Keyboard Commands, at `http://developer.android.com/sdk/installing/studio-tips.html#KeyCommands`

5. *Chapter 5, Creating User Interfaces*:

    ° Layouts, at http://developer.android.com/guide/topics/ui/declaring-layout.html

    ° Input Controls, at http://developer.android.com/guide/topics/ui/controls.html

    ° Input Events, at http://developer.android.com/guide/topics/ui/ui-events.html

    ° Supporting multiple screens, at http://developer.android.com/guide/practices/screens_support.html

6. *Chapter 6, Google Play Services*:

    ° Google Play Services, at http://developer.android.com/google/play-services/

    ° PlusOneButton, at https://developer.android.com/reference/com/google/android/gms/plus/PlusOneButton.html

7. *Chapter 7, Tools*:

    ° SDK Manager, at http://developer.android.com/tools/help/sdk-manager.html

    ° Managing Virtual Devices, at http://developer.android.com/tools/devices/

8. *Chapter 8, Debugging*:

    ° Using DDMS, at http://developer.android.com/tools/debugging/ddms.html

    ° Reading and Writing Logs, at http://developer.android.com/tools/debugging/debugging-log.html

    ° Profiling with Traceview and dmtracedump, at http://developer.android.com/tools/debugging/debugging-tracing.html

9. *Chapter 9, Preparing for Release*:

    ° Publishing Overview, at http://developer.android.com/tools/publishing/publishing_overview.html

Updates

From the help menu we can check for updates of Android Studio. Navigate to **Help | Check for Update**. When the checking finishes, if there is an available update of Android Studio we have not installed, the update info is shown in a dialog box. This dialog box is shown in the next screenshot. We can look over our current version, the new version code, and its size. We can choose if we want to ignore the update, update it later (**Remind Me Later** button), review the online release notes about the update (**Release Notes** button), or install the update (**Update and Restart** button). Click on this last option to update Android Studio. The update starts to download first, then Android Studio will restart and the update will be installed.

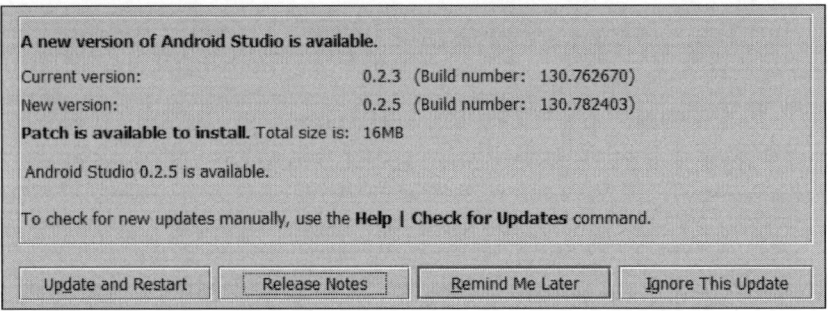

If we already have the latest version of Android Studio, the following message will be shown:

You already have the latest version of Android Studio (I/O Preview) installed. To configure automatic update settings, see the Updates dialog of your IDE settings

Click on the **Updates** link to open the updates configuration dialog. We can select if we want Android Studio to automatically check for updates and what type of updates to check, for example, beta releases or stable releases.

We can examine the information about the recent Android Studio updates by navigating to the menu **Help | What's New in Android Studio**. This information is available online at `http://tools.android.com/recent`. To get the current version we have of Android Studio or even the Java version in our system, navigate to **Help | About**.

Summary

We have learned how to use the Android Studio documentation in case we need help with any action available in the IDE. We have also learned about the update feature to always have the latest version of Android Studio installed. By the end of this chapter, the user should be able to search for help using the online documentation and the help topics, and to keep their Android Studio updated with the latest features at their disposal.

Index

Ctrl + Y 31
Shift + Ctrl + Arrows 31
Tab 31
Show in Explorer button 81
signed APK
generating 80, 81
Smart Keys option 24
smart type code completion 26
Software Development Kit Manager. *See*
SDK Manager
src/main/ 20
Start button 59
Start Tracking button 73
Stop Tracking button 73
String parameter 26
system information tab, DDMS 74

T

Tab 31
Target SDK field 12
Test option 29
text-based editor 35, 36
Text Fields 35
text option 37
TextView.setText method 71
TGZ file
for Linux systems, URL 6
Theme field 12

threads tab, DDMS 70
troubleshooting
URL 84
tv_greeting object 68
Type Hierarchy option 30

U

uiCompass 52
UI theme
changing 41, 42
uiZoomControls 52
Update from Device button 74
updates
of Android Studio 86

V

VCS 62, 63
Version Control option 21
Version control system. *See* **VCS**
View class 42
View object 43
v method 68

W

Widgets 35
w method 68

Thank you for buying
Android Studio Application Development

About Packt Publishing

Packt, pronounced 'packed', published its first book "*Mastering phpMyAdmin for Effective MySQL Management*" in April 2004 and subsequently continued to specialize in publishing highly focused books on specific technologies and solutions.

Our books and publications share the experiences of your fellow IT professionals in adapting and customizing today's systems, applications, and frameworks. Our solution based books give you the knowledge and power to customize the software and technologies you're using to get the job done. Packt books are more specific and less general than the IT books you have seen in the past. Our unique business model allows us to bring you more focused information, giving you more of what you need to know, and less of what you don't.

Packt is a modern, yet unique publishing company, which focuses on producing quality, cutting-edge books for communities of developers, administrators, and newbies alike. For more information, please visit our website: www.packtpub.com.

About Packt Open Source

In 2010, Packt launched two new brands, Packt Open Source and Packt Enterprise, in order to continue its focus on specialization. This book is part of the Packt Open Source brand, home to books published on software built around Open Source licences, and offering information to anybody from advanced developers to budding web designers. The Open Source brand also runs Packt's Open Source Royalty Scheme, by which Packt gives a royalty to each Open Source project about whose software a book is sold.

Writing for Packt

We welcome all inquiries from people who are interested in authoring. Book proposals should be sent to author@packtpub.com. If your book idea is still at an early stage and you would like to discuss it first before writing a formal book proposal, contact us; one of our commissioning editors will get in touch with you.

We're not just looking for published authors; if you have strong technical skills but no writing experience, our experienced editors can help you develop a writing career, or simply get some additional reward for your expertise.

Android User Interface Development: Beginner's Guide

ISBN: 978-1-84951-448-4   Paperback: 304 pages

Quickly design and develop compelling user interfaces for your Android applications

1. Leverage the Android platform's flexibility and power to design impactful user-interfaces.

2. Build compelling, user-friendly applications that will look great on any Android device.

3. Make your application stand out from the rest with styles and themes.

4. A practical Beginner's Guide to take you step-by-step through the process of developing user interfaces to get your applications noticed!.

Android 4: New Features for Application Development

ISBN: 978-1-84951-952-6   Paperback: 166 pages

Develop Android applications using the new features of Android Ice Cream Sandwich

1. Learn new APIs in Android 4.

2. Get familiar with the best practices in developing Android applications.

3. Step-by-step approach with clearly explained sample codes.

Please check **www.PacktPub.com** for information on our titles

Printed in Great Britain
by Amazon.co.uk, Ltd.,
Marston Gate.